Let us reason
TOGETHER!

BY LEROY CANNADY

ISBN: 978-1-4951-3270-4

Printed by LifeSprings Resources

Franklin Springs, Georgia

Dear Leroy,

Of all the stories, group therapy, etc., I've participated in since I've been in the treatment center, your personal story touched me the most. I am so grateful you shared it today. I'm also envious of the relationship you have with Jesus Christ.

I've tried for years to stay on the straight and narrow path. I not only believe but also know with all my heart that Christ is the "LIGHT" and the Way, but I continue to relapse.

I am 40 years old, and here I am. I've lost two husbands and four children because I am a weak woman. I am leaving today to go back out into the world and try again. Maybe your daughter can say a prayer of deliverance for me!

I was hurting so much on the inside and feeling that life was empty. Thank you for your inspiration!

Sincerely,
Beverly

....

Brother Leroy,

Just a note of thanks to you for allowing God to use you in telling your testimony. On Sunday, September 29, when you visited my Church in Chattanooga, TN, to share your story, my family was in turmoil.

You see, we have a 20-year-old son that is currently wayward and has a story so similar to yours. He, too, was a "reject" from the military. Now, he has begun a life of drugs and alcohol. The Sunday you came, my husband and I had decided that we would take our son and these issues to the altar to surrender them to Christ. We did just that and as our family knelt to pray, you stood over us and prayed!!

God used you because the very things you prayed were the things we were planning to surrender! We are so thankful for your testimony! We know that God is faithful, and we trust His Word.

So by this hope, we are confident that our son will return to Christ and may someday tell his testimony as you have done! This is proof of the confirmation of God's love, grace, and mercy! Please continue to lift my family in prayer.

Thank you, and may the Lord Jesus Christ continue to bless you and your testimony!

The Family of Kenneth and Erika

SPECIAL RECOGNITION

This book is dedicated to three women who made a noticeable difference in both my life and all my children's lives.

A PRAYING AUNT: She continued to pray for me even after I caused her some embarrassing moments by stealing money from her church. She told me many times, "Lee, Jesus has a plan for your life.!"

A PRAYING WIFE: She married me in spite of my drugs, lying, cheating, and alcoholic condition. She prayed and told me, "Jesus can change your life!"

A PRAYING DAUGHTER: "Dad, this morning in Sunday School, I prayed that you would quit smoking (2 packs a day)!" At that moment, I got sick to my stomach at the smell of cigarettes!

The Lord Jesus Christ heard their prayers, and each one of them witnessed the results.

Special thanks to Ashley Adams (from Philadelphia, PA), Jean Nicholson (from Winston Salem, NC), and Phyllis Synan (from Franklin Springs, GA).

ALSO I HEARD THE VOICE OF THE LORD, SAYING WHOM SHALL I SEND, AND WHO WILL GO FOR US? THEN SAID I, HERE AM I; SEND ME. AND HE SAID, GO AND TELL THIS PEOPLE... ."

But Jesus said, *Suffer little children, and forbid them not, to come unto me: for of such is the kingdom of heaven. Matthew 19:14, KJV*

They were hungry and without clothing but the church ministered to their needs, physically and spiritually.

OUR MISSION: To see men, women, boys, and girls come to a saving knowledge of Jesus Christ!

We encourage new believers to find a church body who believes and teaches that the Bible, in its entirety, is the inspired Word of God.

As a believer, we have the assurance of Romans 10:9: *"That if thou shalt confess with thy mouth the Lord Jesus, and believe in thine heart that God hath raised him from the dead, thou shalt be saved."*

Leroy Cannady is available for any speaking events.

- Church services, Men's, Women's, Youth, Pastoral Meetings, Banquets, and Conventions.

- Jail and Prison Ministry, Homeless and Missionary outreaches.

- His message will focus on the events of his life and how the Lord Jesus Christ changed it for His glory.

For ordering and scheduling, please contact Leroy at

www.leroycannady.com

CONTENTS

I.   Without Reason 7

II. Finding Reason.................................. 96

III. Living Reason: With God 104

I. WITHOUT REASON

THE EARLY YEARS

At the young age of nine, while other kids were playing and engaging in after school activities, I was helping my mother bottle bootleg whiskey every day in the basement. Selling corned whiskey was the means by which she supported our family.

I started to resent my parents at that time because of the bootlegging work I had to do in the basement. Seeing all my friends having fun outside after school made me realize my childhood was different.

My bootlegging bottling work had become so demanding it required me to work late into the night, which meant homework assignments were not completed. I was left behind that year, in the third grade. I remember giving my parents my report card, and my father getting very angry. He said to my mother; "THIS BOY IS DRIVING ME TO DRINK!" And that's exactly what he did. He had a reason to take another drink.

My father got drunk that night and beat me with his belt while my brother and sister looked on. He turned around and looked at them, and said, "THIS IS WHAT YOU'LL GET IF YOU BRING HOME A REPORT CARD LIKE THIS!"

My sister, who was eight, was so frightened, she ran into the other room and began crying profusely. My little brother, age six, sat in the corner shaking like a leaf on a tree during a windstorm. I had never seen my brother and sister so afraid as I saw them that night.

The school that I attended was located on the corner of 17th and Norris Street in North Philadelphia. The school was located by an old cemetery that dated back to the 1700s, but to the kids in my town, it was a shortcut to get home quickly. Most of my friends took the same route home, and we would stop along the way to play on the old gravestones and swing on the vines that had grown up around the tombstones and trees.

On more than one occasion, someone would fall into one of the open vaults and injure himself, but that didn't stop us from taking the shortcut home. Usually on this shortcut, there were fights along the way.

One day a fight broke out between two other kids and me. The police arrived quickly to break up the fight. My anger was deep because of the resentment I was feeling toward my parents for the work I had to perform in the cellar. I kicked one of the police officers in the groin. The other three officers immediately grabbed me and beat me to the ground. They beat me with their night sticks and black jacks until blood was coming from my head, my nose, my arms, and leg. I took my anger out on those police officers, and I paid the price. To this day, I am carrying the marks on my body from those police officers.

One day we were taking the shortcut home when a young girl went missing. She fell into one of the open graves. It took days of searching before they could find her body. Her family did not know if she had run away or been kidnapped. Shortly after this incident, the city closed our graveyard shortcut. Then, a few years later, all the bodies from the graveyard were relocated, and Temple University built a football-training field on that site.

I was glad when the university took over because it gave me something to look at while I worked in the cellar bottling whiskey. I loved watching the college students while they had their football practice and track meets because that was the most entertainment we had in our neighborhood other than the common street fights we would see.

Sports were something I never had an opportunity to get involved in during my school days because of my afternoon duties at home. When my friends got together and talked about sports, I always felt out of place.

Both of my parents were alcoholics. I had the greatest father anyone could ever ask for, until he started drinking. He used to take us to the other side of town to watch him play half ball with his friends. Half ball was a big game in Philly during that time. It starts by cutting a tennis ball in half, and a broomstick is used as a bat. The teams consist of 3-5 players depending on the area. Those were some great moments in my life, but when my father started drinking, he was a different person. Sometimes he would take his belt, tie it around my neck, and make my brother ride on my back like riding a horse. If I complained, he would put the belt around my neck and pull me across the floor like a dog on a noose. My mother would tell him in her quiet voice, "James, leave the kids alone." However, if she were drinking, nothing would be said, but she would laugh because she found it amusing as well.

During the long days of summer, we played basketball in the neighborhood. We did not have a regular basketball goal as kids have today. We made our own from a piece of plywood as the backboard and wire basket or wooden milk crates with the bottom cut out for the hoop. We then nailed the basket to the backboard and nailed the backboard to the telephone pole. No one in the neighborhood could afford to buy anything close to a basketball goal, and the only other place you could play basketball was in the schoolyard. However, the schoolyard closed immediately after school hours. Some of us would climb the schoolyard fence, but that was short-lived because the police would come and chase us away.

One day while we were outside playing basketball, my little brother Frank had a problem holding onto the ball with his right hand. His teammates yelled at him constantly, asking him to stop dropping the ball and turning it over to the other team. Frank would laugh and tell them he wasn't doing it on purpose. He just didn't have any control of his right hand. Frank was about 8 years old at the time.

My mother noticed later that night how Frank could not hold his pencil to write his homework. The following day she took him to the clinic, where he was tested and diagnosed with sickle-cell-anemia (a muscle disease). From that point on, I watched my brother Frank go from a healthy 8-year-old to skin and bones. Within a few years, he died. My anger toward God burned deep inside of me because of the loss of my baby brother, my best friend during those days.

Following my brother's death, I stayed in the house for weeks playing games and pretending he was the other player. Neither one of my parents noticed how his death was affecting my social skills because they were too drunk.

My brother's death took a toll on both my parents. They buried themselves deeper in alcohol. Shortly afterward, my father was drinking so much he could not go to work, which in turn, made him lose his job. He continued to drink even more than he did before that happened. He drank every day, from morning till night....more- more- more!

My mother was drinking just as much, but she managed to maintain enough sense to sustain her bootleg whiskey business. That was the only way we had enough money to put food on the table. There were times when she couldn't afford to pay cash and buy us clothes for school or for special holidays, like Easter or Christmas, so she bought them on credit from the Jewish-owned stores in the neighborhood. Everyone knew everyone in the neighborhood, so credit wasn't an issue, because people didn't move as often as they do today. I remember how some stores had a man who came around each week to collect the payments. The only problem with that method was you paid three times the value of items you purchased.

The tension in our home continued to grow over our

finances and the loss of my brother so that my sister began suffering great depression.

During those days, there were no social programs to help deal with the grief and depression one was going through. We had to rely on family members and close friends to help us through these trying times. My sister's situation was just another hurt that was added to my ever growing anxiety, and it was during that time that I developed a deeper resentment toward God.

My parents became very argumentative and resentful toward each other during the months following my brother's death. They were always at each other, cursing, name calling, and blaming each other for our circumstances. I began to develop the same attitude, and their curse words became a part of my vocabulary in school toward my teachers and classmates.

My anger continued to build, and the empty feelings in my life continued to grow even more. I didn't have anyone that I could talk with about my anger and the resentful feelings I had toward God and my parents. I tried to hide these deep within. I was hurting so badly, I would bury my head in my pillow at night and engage in a hard cry to ease my pain.

When I woke up in the morning, my eyes were blood shot and stayed that way most of the school day. I got into an argument during the gym hour one day when two kids made fun of my red eyes. I waited until they got into the shower, and I beat both of them with a baseball bat. They were taken to the hospital. I was taken to jail and later suspended. When I got home later that day, my father tried to beat me with his belt, but he was too drunk. I dodged all his swings until he was exhausted. After a while, he gave up and got himself another drink and passed out.

THE DAY MY WORLD COLLAPSED

It was approaching the Christmas Season, and my mother was concerned about our financial situation. I heard her talking to my father about his drinking and how he was chasing her business away. She reminded him that this was our only source of income and his drinking had chased away some of her best customers. She told him how some of her most dependable customers didn't come around anymore, and it was the result of his drinking and foul mouth.

He got very upset over her comments. He hit her, knocking her to the floor and he began kicking her violently. We didn't have a phone, so I ran to our neighbor's house and called the police. He was arrested, but released a few days later. The following week the incident repeated itself when he got drunk, but this time he got thirty days in the county jail. When he came home, he was like a new man. We were happy because we had our father back. He was level-headed and sober.

It was the day after Christmas. My parents had been drinking heavily during the holidays, and they continued their ritual of getting angry and blaming each other for our living conditions. My mother told my father that she was sick of the arguments and fighting; therefore, she was taking us kids and moving in with her sister. He became extremely angry over her comments. He slapped her very hard and she fell back across the table. He hit her again and she fell across the bed where we were lying.

When she got up, she grabbed a knife and started swinging so violently, we had to get out of the way. It had turned into a street fight. My father was hit by the knife several times, and he fell slowly to the floor holding his chest. None of us knew what to say, so we watched as he lay there on the floor without any sound or movement. Everything became very quiet and still.

My mother screamed, "I think he's dead, kids...... I know he's dead!! O GOD, WHAT HAVE I DONE????

She told my sister Ann to run next door and call the police. When Ann left the house, my mother put the knife in my hand and told me to tell the police that he was beating on her, and I stabbed him to protect her. I was thirteen and my sister was eleven years old when we witnessed the stabbing death of our father.

When the police arrived, I did as I was told. They took my statement and the statement of my mother and sister. Then they went on their way after my father's body was removed.

A few hours later, more police officers returned to interview the neighbors, along with my sister, again. They told my mother that her statement, my statement, and that of my sister didn't match the account of what happened as they conducted their investigation. They asked her once again if she had anything to add to the account of what happened. She said no, and they left.

News of what happened that morning didn't travel as fast as it does today. It was confined to the neighborhood. Our father was dead, and we didn't know what to do. Neighbors were in and out of our house during the day trying to comfort my mother. Everyone was aware of my father's abusive behavior and drinking problems. I can't remember anyone expressing sympathy for his death.

It was getting late and nearing the time for church. My

mother encouraged us kids to go. We got dressed and headed off to church to participate in the Christmas program during the Sunday Evening Service. The church service was in full swing, and the place was packed. We were singing Christmas carols when the doors at the back of the church opened. It got everyone's attention because of the noise. The doors in the center of the church had been nailed closed to keep down distractions when people arrived late. The police officers were not aware of this so they pushed the doors open and caused a large commotion.

Once the doors opened, there stood four white police officers in uniform in an all-black church. This got everyone's attention. One officer said in a very loud voice, "We are looking for Leroy Cannady!"

Every eye turned toward me as I stood there. The police officers walked in my direction, and they told me that I was under arrest for the murder of my father. You could hear the mumbling of the crowd as they handcuffed me and led me out of the church. My mother and sister broke down and began crying loudly out of control. The other kids in the church were scared, and they began crying also. I cannot imagine how the rest of the Christmas program went that evening after that horrifying scene.

When I arrived at the police station, they did what police officers do when someone is charged with a crime. I was crying all the time while going through the booking process because it was frightening to me. After the booking process, they placed me in a small room by myself. The wait time seemed like hours.

Later, a police officer came into the room and offered me something to drink. I refused the drink and told him that all I wanted was to go home to my family. He said that would be possible if I told him the truth and that meant telling him the whole story.

I replied by saying "I did tell the truth this afternoon and that was the whole story." He replied in a loud tone, "STOP LYING TO ME, BOY!!"

At that time, I lost it and I started crying, pulling my hair and pacing the floor. He yelled at me again and told me to sit down and shut up!

He waited a few minutes, and then he told me he was going to put me in lockup with the other inmates. He walked out of the room and shortly afterward, another officer came in and took me to a cell that was occupied by other inmates who were much older than I was.

I stopped crying because I was relieved that I was out of that room with those detectives. The older inmates in that cell were staring at me and smiling.

One of them asked me, "You want to be my bitch? I love young boys!" Then another inmate smiled and said, "Let me have him when you're finished!"

Both of them were big men and each of them had a smile on his face that led me to believe that they were as serious as a heart attack when referring to what they were going to do to me when they had the chance.

A short time later, one inmate grabbed me and put me in a bear hug. He lifted me off the floor and tried to kiss me. Everyone was cheering him on. I didn't know what to do, but one thing I knew for sure, I was not going to let him make a *woman* out of me without a fight. So I put my arms around his neck and squeezed it tight while he still had me in a bear hug. Then I bit a portion of his ear off and spat it in his face.

He grabbed his ear and started screaming for help. The other inmates saw what happened and one of them called the guards. I backed away into a corner of the cell block and positioned myself like a ball as I sat on the floor. I was scared to death of what the other inmates may do to me. I was tired, but I was too afraid to fall asleep. From that point forward, the inmates started calling me, **"MAD DOG!"**

It wasn't long until another detective came to the cell and escorted me to another room. He asked me "Are you ready to talk to me now, boy?" I said yes! At that point, the police officer was my best friend. I was shaking like a leaf as I rushed to the front of the cell. He cuffed me and led me down the hallway to another one of those small rooms that resembled the one I was in before.

We passed a room with a big dark window, and that's when I saw my mother sitting at a table talking to another detective. I was not aware that she was there. I burst into tears and called out to her for help. The police officer told me she couldn't hear or see me because it was a thick one-way mirror.

This was the first time in my life that I can ever remember asking God for anything. I prayed, "Lord, if you are real, please help us! I cannot understand what's happening to my family. Please help us, Lord!!"

A short time later, a detective came into my room and told me someone would take me home. I was confused but relieved. I didn't understand why they had such a sudden change of heart and attitude.

Later I learned my mother broke down and told them exactly what happened, and her statement lined up with their investigation. She pleaded self-defense and based on my father's background of abuse, my mother didn't serve any time.

Once I was released from jail, I became even more angry and bitter. The Lord had answered my prayers, and I didn't even realize it. I was caught up in my own world of self-pity, anger, and bitterness.

A NEW BEGINNING

My life took on new meaning after the death of my father. I became heavily involved with drugs, alcohol, and prostitution.

There was a man who owned a meat store in my neighborhood by the name of Charlie K. He gave me a job in his meat store to help keep me out of trouble with the law and to help keep the local gangs from breaking into his meat store and stealing merchandise.

Charlie and I became very good friends. He was like the father I never had but longed for. He lived just outside the city of Philadelphia in a town named Media.

I would go out to his house on Sundays and spend the entire day with him and his wife. Charlie and I would cut the grass, wash the cars, and play cards until Mrs. K called us in for lunch. Doing these things with Charlie made me feel so good inside. This was a new experience for me because I wasn't used to sitting down eating a meal with anyone, not even at home. It was obvious to them that I didn't have any table manners, but they patiently helped me to improve in that area.

During the weekdays, I continued to work after school with my mother, bottling whiskey, but on weekends I worked at the Penn Beef Company with Charlie. I met a lot of nice people who shopped in the store, and some of them became some of my closest friends.

One of the people I met was a lady by the name of Gloria. She was in her mid-thirties, married and had two girls under the age of three. Gloria came shopping every day to pick up what she needed for dinner.

Shopping daily was a normal habit of people back in those days because most homes only had very small refrigerators with no freezer space. Most families got their milk, eggs, bread, and butter delivered directly to their homes early in the morning. Then they would shop daily at the local markets for their fresh vegetables and meats.

Gloria and I became very close, and we started having an affair. She was much older than I was. After all, I was only fifteen. Gloria schooled me in all the different ways that I could make money in dealing drugs and using my body for sex. She was my teacher, and I followed her instructions to the letter of the law, and it worked!

After a while, Charlie caught me red-handed dealing drugs across the counter to his customers, and he was furious!

I didn't believe he could get that upset over what I did. But after all, my action was a violation of trust because I had told him and Mrs. K. that I had stopped using and dealing drugs. I was lost for words over his anger. I knew at that moment there was nothing that I could say to ease his hurt. He fired me that day. Our tightly knit relationship came to an end.

A few months later, Charlie sold his store, and that was the last time we saw each other. Losing Charlie as a father figure left an enormous void in my life. However, I buried my pain by using more drugs and moving forward in life. After all, I had become a master when it came to hiding my hurt and pain.

Working with Charlie in his butcher shop during my teenage years became the foundation for my career as a meat cutter, and later as a cattle buyer.

On the other side, Gloria and I continued our drugs and prostitution working relationship for about a year, but we eventually drifted apart. By that time, she had taught me enough to venture out on my own. I was the king pin of drugs and prostitution in my North Philadelphia neighborhood.

I was getting involved in so many illegal things during the summer that it caught the attention of my mother. She feared that I would end up in jail. So she sent me to live with my grandfather in Montgomery, Alabama.

A BREAK FROM THE ACTION

When I was younger, I used to love going south and spending a few weeks on the farm of my grandfather. I would love going fishing, helping in the field, and the big cookouts they had every Sunday after church. That was so much fun back then! Now, I had outgrown those things because I loved the excitement and fast life of the city.

That morning when my mother put me on that Greyhound Bus, the thought of running away became very real to me. But my biggest fear was loneliness.

It was a very long ride on that bus, but I met a young

lady when we stopped in D.C. She was going to Atlanta, Georgia. I could tell by the burn marks on her fingertips that she got high. I started the conversation about getting high, and she ran with it. When we made our first stop in Virginia, we got off the bus and got high as kites. We were stoned out of our minds, giggling and talking loud. She was not aware that I was only fifteen years old. A few hours later when our journey commenced, we moved to the rear of the bus for privacy. When we arrived in Atlanta, she was greeted by an older man. I knew he wasn't her father because she kissed him as she had kissed me on the bus. However, she gave me big hug and a few joints for the rest of my trip.

When I arrived in Montgomery, my grandfather was at the station. He was driving his horse and buggy. Earlier in my life, this was an exciting ride, but not now. My grandfather was not big on conversation, but that was fine with me; I was still deep in thought of the lady I met on the trip.

My grandfather didn't have any plans for us, but there was a new family who had moved into the farmhouse across the street. They had two boys my age and a younger sister. We hit if off really well from the start.

They didn't smoke weed, but they turned me on to some tobacco that was stronger than any cigarette that I had ever smoked. After smoking one of those cigarettes, my head was spinning like a spinning top, and I was on cloud nine for hours.

One Saturday morning, we walked a few miles to the main street to catch the bus going downtown. That was the only day we could go to the movie theater. I was excited to know there was something to do off the farm.

When the bus pulled up, I was about to step on, but my friend said that I had to let the white people get on first. I asked, "Why?" He said, "That's the way it is down here." My friend held my shirt to hold me back. I didn't have any knowledge at of all the racial issues that were going on in the South.

When I got on the bus, my friends went straight to the back of the bus. I didn't. I grabbed a seat up front! I was not expecting the driver's response; "HEY NIGGER, GET YOUR ASS TO THE BACK!"

My friends ran up front and grabbed my arm pulling me toward the back of the bus before I could say a word. I did not realize the consequences of my action. Where I came from, I could ride the bus and subway and sit anywhere I pleased. Later that day, I learned that was not the case in Alabama. That incident left me in a state of anger for days.

I wrote my mother and I explained what happened and asked her, why? After my mother received my letter, she sent a telegram to my grandfather, asking him to send me home ASAP. He did!

GOING HOME

When I got back to Philly, I was happy to be home and to see my friends. I asked my mother why I had to come home so soon.

She replied, "The questions you're asking could cost you your life."

She went on to explain all the racial issues that existed in the South which didn't exist in the North. She would never let me go to the South again.

When I got back in Philly, I picked up where I left off with my drug deals. After all, Charlie had fired me for selling drugs across the counter to his customers.

A PRAYING AUNT

My aunt Alberta was a sweet God-loving old lady with whom I could talk about anything. I walked thirteen blocks to her house in the rain to talk to her about why Charlie fired me. She knew about Charlie and our relationship and how he had become a father figure to me. She made mention earlier how I had improved with my manners but not my street habits.

I got to her house that afternoon soaking wet. She opened the door and saw the look on my face. She said "I hope this is not what I think it is" (running from the law). Two of her greatest fears for me were going to jail or getting killed. I explained to her what had happened between Charlie and me, and she prayed at that moment asking the Lord to give me wisdom and direction for my life.

She advised me to start going to church with her. I agreed, but I did not show up the first Sunday. The following Sunday, she came over to my house, pulled me out of bed, and dragged me to church. She told me that she would do this every Sunday until I got my life right with God. I knew she meant every word she spoke, so I decided it would be in my best interest to be ready for church when she arrived.

After a while, church became fun for me because I met some nice young Christian girls and even learned where they put the money from the Sunday School collection plate. I started stealing money from the collection plate to support my drug habits. My friend Reggie rebuked me for taking the money, but I supplied him with drugs in order to keep him quiet. Everything was going great until I got greedy and started taking all the bills from the Sunday School collection and leaving only the change.

One Sunday, a young girl in my Sunday School Class caught me taking the money, and she turned me in to the elders of the church. The church elders took me to this place they called the "UPPER ROOM." They told me that I should repent and possibly do some work around the church to help repay the money that was taken. I agreed to do what they asked so they wouldn't turn me in to the police. However, when I left that church, they never ever saw me again!

The biggest regret that I had when I left that church was the hurt and embarrassment it caused my Aunt Alberta. The following week when she came over to my house, she gave me a big hug without saying any words of conviction. She looked me straight in the eye and said with a smile, "The Lord will forgive you if you ask and so will I." She never mentioned what took place in the church to my mother or anyone else outside the church.

As I got older, she would always call or send me a message that she was praying for me. My Aunt Alberta attended that church, serving the Lord, until the day she died twelve years later. She never lived to see the results of the seed she planted in my life.

As I look back now, I am reminded of the encouraging words she used to share with me how the Lord had a plan for my life;

Jeremiah 29:11: *"For I know the plans I have for you,"* *declares the Lord, "plans to prosper you and not to harm you, plans to give you hope and a future."*

Thank you, Lord, for loving and knowing me when I didn't even know myself!!

LIFE GOES ON

My mother never worked a day in her life, but she made a very good living hustling and selling bootleg whiskey. Although she was a very good provider, she fell short on motherhood. All of us were put on auto pilot growing up. My home life was like living in a barroom every day. The smell of alcohol and the sight of drunks lying on the floor and sitting around my dining room table every day were sickening. There were days when I came home from school that I had to wait before I could go into my room because my mother had rented it out for sexual activities. That didn't bother me too much because I knew it was just another way of her making money. I hated the fact that I had to clean up the mess they made in bed so I could sleep in it after they were finished.

One day my mother told us she was getting married to a man name Stanley. We were excited because all of us liked Stanley. He had a good job and didn't drink like the others who came over to the house. Stanley would stop by on occasion to have a drink before going to work, but I never saw him drunk like his friends.

On some occasions, when Stanley came over, he would give me a few dollars so I could attend the weekly dance at the skating ring on Saturday nights. He didn't talk much to my sister so she kept her distance. Although we were excited about the wedding, we didn't know what to expect concerning our home life.

Ann and I would lie awake at night talking about how we were going to have a real family life from now on with Stanley in the house. Both of us wanted a father and mother like most of the other kids had.

Both of us admired some of the kids in our neighborhood who had two parents living together. I thought everything would change for the better when my mother and Stanley got married. However, it went in the opposite direction. Our house became one big party room every day during their first month of marriage. Everyone was coming by to celebrate with the newlyweds. After all it was free food, free liquor, and plenty of women hanging around for the men to dance with. Stanley even hired a DJ to spin records. It was one big party every single day and night. However, when the free food and liquor stopped, the crowd stopped coming. Stanley didn't like that. He wanted the party to continue on like before. However, my mother wanted to get back to her business and she wanted Stanley to go back to work.

Since the crowd was not coming to the house, Stanley started buying liquor with his own money so his "friends" would continue to hang around. Within a few short months after they got married, Stanley started drinking like the rest of the crowd. He was always too drunk to work, so he had to use all his vacation and sick time, eventually losing his job.

All that seniority, the good pay, and the benefits he had went down the drain. His friend would tell him, "Don't worry, Gussie (my mother's name) is making good money, and she'll take care of you."

Stanley really believed that my mother loved him so much that he didn't have to work. Stanley didn't know my mother as well as he thought. She was a cold hearted person when it came to parting with her money.

I couldn't believe someone could give up such a good job like that and change so quickly after he started drinking. There were men who would do anything to have a job working in that auto factory, but not him. He was fired for not going to work.

Mom and Stanley would argue big time over his drinking and losing his job. Their arguments reminded my sister and me of the days when our father was alive. We had a great fear of the outcome because we didn't want anything to happen to our mother.

HE WAS NO FATHER FIGURE

Stanley became a burden to all of us, and we resented his being in our house. There were times when he was so drunk, I had to carry him upstairs to bed. He would pass out on the floor in front of my friends and my mother's customers. I'm sure my mother thought once she got married to Stanley, our lives were going to change for the better because Stanley had the qualities to be a good family man and provider for our family.

I noticed the disappointment in her face whenever he walked into the room. She would just take another drink and go on about her business.

Stanley had a set of friends who loved to gamble when they stopped by to have a drink. My mother gave him an idea, "Why don't you turn one of the bedrooms into a gambling room?" After all, they had stopped sleeping together, so she suggested using their room as a gambling hall.

Everything worked out great once he got sober and got things started. Men and women came from all over North Philly to play cards and shoot craps all night. The only winner was the house, because the house got 10% of every pot, big or small.

My mother's bootleg whiskey business really increased during that time. There were so many people going in and out of our house that it caught the attention of the local police! But my mother being the business woman she was, jumped right up and paid them off. The local police became some of her best customers for whiskey and the young women.

ON MY OWN

It was getting cold, and I wanted something to do to make money for myself without hanging out on the corners at night, so I got in on the action by cleaning out the basement and started having weekend parties for my friends. After all, there was no place for us teenagers to hang out except the skating rink on weekends and they closed at 10 p.m., and we had to be off the streets by 11 p.m. But now we had a place where we could party, dance, drink, and smoke weed like the grownups. After all, my mother was upstairs doing her own thing; Stanley was on the second floor doing his thing; so I was on my own.

Some of the young girls who came over would hit on the older men for paid sex and drinks and that added another dimension to my mother's money-making scheme.

Most of the women were only drinking water with lemon, but the men paid my mother for a glass of liquor. She gave the young women a few dollars for their effort encouraging the men to buy them drinks. My part of the business went on for a while but faded out as kids got older and went off to high school.

MUSTANG SALLY

My mother was doing very well in her business, but she never had a bank account or established any credit. One day she decided to buy a new car, but she didn't have a Driver's License nor did she know how to drive a car. Her urge to buy a new car was motivated by the hit song that came out that year ("Mustang Sally"). She was determined to get herself a Mustang.

I'm not sure of the details of how she pulled it off to purchase a new car, but she came home one day with a brand new yellow 1965 Mustang. It was nice! Everyone, including family and grandchildren all called her "Mustang Sally." My next-door neighbor was her driver. That car would sit in front of the house for days without moving. When she wanted to go somewhere, she didn't let Stanley nor me drive her car. She hired our next-door neighbor Nat to drive her every place she wanted to go. Nat drove her to shop down in the Italian Market on weekdays, and she went to the clubs in Long Side, New Jersey, on Sundays. That car didn't move unless she was in it and Nat was driving. Most of the time it was filled with her party friends, but she picked up the tab most of the time. Most of her friends didn't work and were on welfare.

Nat loved being around my mother because he could travel in style, drinking as much as he liked, getting paid at the same time. It was a win-win situation for both of them. After eleven years of ownership, she had accumulated fewer than 9000 miles on that Mustang. Other than the smell of alcohol and cigarettes, it looked just as good as the day she brought it home from the dealer.

IN TROUBLE AGAIN

One day my mother received a call from the Vice Principal at my school because of problems that I was having in school. I remember on one occasion she had to attend a parent conference on my behalf. She and Stanley walked into the classroom, both of them so drunk they had to hold each other up. My mother started cursing at the teacher and said how they were picking on me because of her activities in the home. There were a few teachers who were some of her best customers, and when my mother's back was up against the wall, she would call you out, big time.

I was never so embarrassed in all my life when other parents and teachers stopped what they were doing to listen to her run her mouth. She got so loud they had to call some of the male teachers to escort them out of the building, but she didn't stop cursing. She pulled me out of school that day and took me home with them.

On the way home, she said she was transferring me to another school. That was the last thing I wanted to hear! I was in the last half of the ninth grade in this school and was already a grade behind, and she wanted to take me out. I wanted to graduate from that school so I could attend a high school of my choice in the city. After she settled down, I appealed to Stanley for help. He talked to her, and she agreed to let me finish the school year at that school.

During the summer before I entered high school, I really struggled with drugs and alcohol. I was selling and using weed and cocaine in a big way. I felt lost, lonely, and without purpose. I thought maybe I needed more drugs or more money — just more — more of anything to fill the emptiness that was in my life.

A NEW BEGINNING

I got a job working in a meat market located in South Philadelphia in the Italian market district of South Philly. That was a rewarding move because that's where I met Tony Alberto who later became my best friend. We worked in the same meat market, and we became the salt and pepper team of the Italian market. During the fall, we attended the same high school in South Philly, and the kids looked up to us because we supplied them with whatever drugs they needed.

We spent weekends in each other's homes, and both our mothers took a liking to our relationship. His mother thought I was a good influence for him, and my mother thought the same. Little did they know what was really going on in our lives.

Tony had two brothers who were police officers, and they knew we were dealing drugs. They did a great job keeping us out of big-time trouble with the law. Of course their services weren't free! There were some kickbacks which included supplying them with drugs and sex with some of our high school girlfriends. It became a win-win relationship for all of us.

Later in the fall, when the school year started, Tony and I found ourselves in the same homeroom in the tenth grade. Some of the upper class Italian kids wanted to buy corn whiskey for their weekend parties. This kind of whiskey was new to most of them, and they loved it! So I would bring small bottles to school and store them in my locker-- then sell them during recess.

A few months into the school year, I got into an argument with one of the teachers over my business. I was in the middle of transacting a business deal with a few students when I got caught by one of the teachers who was monitoring the halls. The other kids took off running; however, the teacher knew who they were. When he looked in my locker and saw the whiskey, his eyes lit up like a Christmas tree. He escorted me to his office and threatened to call the police if I didn't answer all his questions. The type of questions he was asking led me to believe that he was not going to turn me in to the police or anyone else.

He started getting real personal, and he explained how I could double my sales with his help. He tried to hit me up for a piece of the action, but he wanted 50% of the action. He really pissed me off when he said that. It took every muscle in my body to maintain my cool. Thoughts of how this Jewish fellow was trying to rip me off were racing through my mind at 100 mph. I knew I had to hold myself together because I didn't want to go to jail, so I agreed to his deal. He said we would meet the following day to fine-tune the details.

When I walked out of his office that afternoon, I had one thought and one thought only: "DON'T GET MAD, GET EVEN!"

Later that day when I met up with Tony, I explained what had happened and what this guy wanted so we could continue to deal drugs and liquor in school. Just as I expected, Tony got pissed over this whole situation. He starting pacing the floor and cursing in Italian. After we calmed down, we got stoned and passed out on the floor in his bedroom.

The following day we told one of Tony's brothers about what happened, and he gave us a plan, which was how to set this teacher up and get him off our backs.

We had one of our female classmates sneak into his office early one morning before school started. We got her to fill his office drawer with small bottles of corn whiskey. She informed her mother of how this teacher was selling whiskey to students. Her mother wasted no time calling the school and reported him to the principal's office. I'm not sure about the details of the investigation, but we did not see this teacher around anymore.

It was approaching spring break, and it was a very hot day. One of the bottles of whiskey that I stored in my locker broke, and the smell of the corn whiskey filled the entire hallway. A teacher who was monitoring the hallway that day knew the smell of corn whiskey, so he turned me in.

When they paged me to report to the office, I went straight to my locker that day and loaded all my belongings, walked out of school while Tony did the same. In other words, both of us quit school that same day after completing only a few months in the tenth grade. Tony and I were seventeen years old, and both of us were two grades behind. There was no reason for us to continue going to school. We knew we would be kicked out anyway. That's what they did with students back then who were troublemakers and aged out, so we quit.

We didn't tell our parents that we quit school. We left home every day as if we were going to school, but instead we hung out at an older friend's house in North Philadelphia. There were four homosexuals and three prostitutes living there. Tony fell madly in love with one of the prostitutes, but she was only using him to supply her with drugs.

She would come into the house sometimes and greet him with a kiss then grab ....well you know what. They would then go into the next room and you could hear them getting it on like "two pigs making bacon!"

Our lives began moving very fast for two seventeen-year-old boys. I don't care to elaborate on the details of our activities during this time.

FROM BABY DOLLS TO BOYS

My sister was growing up quickly into womanhood without the help or advice from my mother or any other female family members. Ann would get so depressed at times that I didn't even want her around me at all. She would wake up in the morning and wear to school what she wore to bed the night before. She looked so bad at times I wouldn't let her walk on the same side of the street with. I told her many times to comb her hair and wash her face, but she would just give me a blank look and go on about her business.

During this stage of deep depression, on one occasion, we had to call the fire department to help talk her down from the roof of our three-story apartment building. Then on another occasion, she was rushed to the hospital from taking an overdose of pills. She had very bad crying spells that made her unable to attend a full day of school. She was under close observation during school hours even when she went to the restroom because of the fear of her taking her own life.

In spite of her depression and suicidal tendencies, she was very smart in school. The times when I needed help with my homework, before I quit school, I would be nice and talk to her. Those seemed like the only times I spoke to her.

Later when she entered high school, boys started to pay attention to her because she was good looking and well built. She met a girl in her class named Carrie. They became very good friends. Carrie and Ann were like two peas in a pod. Ann learned a lot from Carrie about being a young lady and cleaning herself up to look good for the boys.

Carrie had a close loving relationship with her family, and I believe Ann noticed it. That's what motivated her to change. Their friendship, along with Carrie's family atmosphere, is what helped mold my sister into a beautiful young woman.

Ann graduated with flying colors and could have received a scholarship to attend any college she applied for, but her life took on new meaning after she finished high school.

After she graduated, we became much closer. I was now proud to let her hang around me. Ann's first boyfriend was Keith Brody. Keith's sister, Debbie was my girlfriend and every weekend we double dated. Later Ann got married to Keith, but she was divorced twice by the age of twenty-three. Ann was searching for a family life that she never had, and she wanted something better for her kids.

All five of her kids have a different father. She was searching for love in all the wrong places which left her all alone after many broken promises from her lovers. She raised five children and two grandchildren on her own, and she strove to give them something she never had, a loving home. Ann was very intelligent, but she never used it to start a career. She lived on welfare raising her kids in the same neighborhood where we grew up, North Philadelphia, all her life.

TIMES OF TRANSITION

At the age of eighteen, I knew there had to be a better way of life. One day I met an Army Recruiter, and he convinced me that the Army could be the change that I was looking for and needed. At that point in my life, I was ready for anything other than the way I was living. He worked fast! I was shipped off to Fort Knox, Kentucky, in only a few days. It happened so fast, I didn't even say good-bye to my family. After we arrived at the base and got settled, they let us call home. The sergeant said that this phone call would be the only phone call we would make for the next eight weeks. He was so right, so, he became our mother and father!

This was the first time that I had ever been away from the city of Philadelphia as an adult, but my get-away was short-lived. I met a lady who lived in Louisville, Kentucky, and she worked in the mess hall. During the first ten days of training, we developed a relationship and spent time together in the mess hall after hours. One night she sneaked me off base by hiding me in the trunk of her car. We bought some drugs and went to her house to party most of the night, but I made it back in plenty of time for roll call the next morning. The following week we did the same thing, but this time we got caught. She was fired, and I was given a choice, go to the stockade or take a D.O. discharge. I took the discharge!

When I left the base, we spent a few days together and she pleaded with me to take her to Philly, but that didn't happen. It didn't happen because I didn't know what I was going to do with my own life, and I didn't want the responsibility of supporting her.

Later after I returned home, I ran into the same Army Recruiter who had recruited me in the first place. He told me how disgusted he was with me. I know that if this situation had happened one year later, the army would have put an M-1 in my hand and shipped me off to Vietnam. There I would have most likely been killed alongside many of my close friends who were drafted.

During the conversation with the recruiter, I really didn't want to hear anything he had to say. All I wanted was a drink and some drugs. Besides, I was the one who was hurting deep on the inside, not him. He had a job and a family. I didn't have anything or anyone, but the drugs made me feel like somebody.

My Aunt Alberta told me years earlier that the Lord had a hand in my life even though my lifestyle didn't line up with His word. She would often quote a scripture from Jeremiah 1:5 that said: **"BEFORE I FORMED YOU IN THE WOMB, I KNEW YOU; BEFORE YOU WERE BORN, I SET YOU APART."**

The weekend after I got kicked out of the army, I left Fort Knox. I took the long ride home on that Greyhound back to Philly. I had plenty of time to think about what I was going to do with my life, but I wasn't coming up with answers on how to make it happen. I was lonely and frustrated with my life. I knew something had to change, but I didn't know what or how.

When I got back to Philly, the first person I looked up was my best friend Tony. Tony was working in a slaughter house in the wholesale district of the city. After Tony and I got high, we got caught up on what had happened during the past few months of our lives. I didn't have a job or any place to stay, but his mother invited me to stay with them until I got back on my feet. Tony said he could get me a job working with him in the slaughter house.

I was grateful for his offer to get me a job, but I had never worked in the wholesale end of the meat business, but Tony assured me I could do it.

Tony's mother was glad that I agreed to stay with them for a while. She enjoyed cooking, and I enjoyed eating her Italian meals. When she started clearing the dinner table, Tony would get up and walk away. I would often stay, and she would talk my head off, which later made me learn to get up when Tony got up.

While working in the slaughter house with Tony, I met another young man working there by the name of Joe Frazier. Joe and I became good friends over the months, and during our lunch hours we would sit outside the plant on the benches and talk about our dreams for the future. Joe would try to influence me with his goodness of a lifestyle. He would try encouraging me to come to the gym and train with him. I told him that he was punch drunk, I wasn't interested in boxing.

I tried to encourage him to sell drugs to some of his friends at ring side, but he was too straight to even talk about it. I tried to convince Joe that we could make more money dealing drugs than he could make fighting at these Friday night fights in the city.

Joe didn't listen to me, and he continued his training and went on to win the gold medal in the Olympics. Later he became the heavy weight champ of the world. Me, I continued on with my lifestyle of drugs and alcohol for years to come.

The emptiness in my life was even greater than before. I couldn't figure it out. What is it, what's wrong with me?

At this time, I had a nice apartment, a good job, a great hustle going on with drugs, and nice looking girlfriends who were always around. Yet, I was still feeling like something was missing in my life. I was sick of this empty feeling, but I didn't know what to do about it! All my friends would tell me how lucky I was and how they wished they had the things that I had. I thought, "If they only knew the emptiness of my life, they wouldn't say such things."

By this time I was approaching my twenties, and I noticed a lot of my friends were getting married. Most of them were about five to ten years older than I was, but they didn't know that. They thought I was their age because of my experiences in life.

One weekend I attended a friend's wedding, where I met a lady named Connie Marie. She knocked me off my feet with her smile, charm, and sophisticated way of dressing. I had never met a young woman who carried herself and looked so much like a model. Later I learned that she had just completed modeling and charm school and was then working as a court secretary, which explained her demeanor.

I wanted this lady so badly in more ways than one. She made me feel good all over when we were together and all we did was talk and hold hands. The more we talked, the more we got to know each other, and she agreed to let me take her home. We had to ride two buses and take the subway to her house. Soon we began dating.

From that day forward, every place we went, she caught the attention of all my friends. All the men and women who were in our company were fascinated with her charm, good looks, and sophistication, but I would let everyone know that she was all mine.

My passion grew hot toward her, but she was not giving in to my cheap talk. That's when it occurred to me, "Ask her to marry you, Dummy. Then you can have all of her." After a few months of dating, I asked Connie to marry me. She accepted.

I thought that was the open door for us to start sleeping together. How wrong I was! When we went out with our friends, all she wanted to do was talk about our wedding plans, the same conversation we had each time we were together. The marriage stuff was getting real old to me, so one day I said "Let's get it over with right now. We can save a lot of money in the long run." I told her, "Let's drive down to Maryland and get married today." She quickly agreed, and I was so relieved.

I really thought that Connie was the person who could make my life whole and complete. I thought she was the one person I needed to get my life going in the right direction. She looked, talked and acted like everything that I thought I needed in life to make me happy: love and companionship.

We asked my friend James and his wife to drive us down to Maryland to get married. The entire process was completed in about an hour. Wow, we are married; we are now "Man and Wife!" I felt great! I felt like a load was lifted off my shoulder! After the ceremony, James and his wife wanted us to go bar-hopping to celebrate our wedding day, but I wanted to spend my time with my new bride. We separated from them and went our own way that weekend.

That following Monday she asked off from work for a few days and I did the same. We needed some time to find a place to live, so I suggested we live with my mother for a while until we found a place. My mother was not aware that we had gotten married.

We left Maryland and headed back to Philly to my mother's house. When we got to her house that Monday afternoon, the place was packed. Everyone was drinking and having fun. My friend James and his wife Gail were there having some drinks.

Neither my mother nor anyone else was aware that Connie and I had eloped and gotten married, except James and his wife. When we walked in the door, James jumped up from the table and shouted in a loud voice "I WANT TO OFFER A TOAST TO THE NEWLYWEDS!" At that moment, I knew my mother wasn't drunk any more.

She stood up and said, "Who are the newlyweds?" Then Gail said, "Mustang Sal, meet your new daughter-in-law!"

At that point, everyone in the house cheered us on. However, my mother and my sister were dumfounded. They were not very happy at all. Both of them knew Connie, and they knew of our long-term wedding plans, but this caught them both off guard. Besides, what son would run off and get married and not tell his sister and his mother.

After the cheering calmed down, the crowd settled and my mother asked the question: "Why didn't you tell us you were getting married this weekend?"

My sister was upset also, she replied, "Lee, how could you do this without telling us? You knew I wanted to be a part of your wedding plans! How you could you do this to us?"

At that moment, I realized how hurt and disappointed they were, and I didn't have any words to comfort them. But my quick thinking wife came to my recue. She said, "Mom, you know how tight our money is right now and I'm sure your finances are the same or worse than ours; so we thought we could save money by driving down to Maryland. It only cost us $25. What a saving over what we were going to spend for a big wedding! Now we can invite our friends over to your house; we can have a big reception, and look at how much money you can make selling whiskey instead of spending it on our wedding. So this is our wedding gift to you along with some grandchildren down the road."

I can tell you, my wife got a standing ovation after that speech, and drinks began to flow and the celebration began. I knew my mother and sister didn't fall for that line, but it sounded good and served the purpose for that time.

Our stay with my mother was short-lived because Connie wanted to start our own family and buy a house. I didn't have the money or knowledge of how to do all the things she wanted, but she kept pushing me.

I got a part-time job working evenings so we could afford to rent our first apartment on the avenue. It was small, but she made it very comfortable and homey. During our first year of marriage, Connie got pregnant. We were filled with joy when our first son was born. Connie planned the pregnancy of each one of our sons. I was a proud father, and I loved taking my sons with me when I visited my friends.

During the first few years of our marriage, we had some lumps and bruises, but we managed to pull through them. Most of the problems we had were financial because I started to gamble playing poker. There were times when I lost my entire paycheck in only a few hours after getting paid. Sometime, I would borrow money from the loan sharks and repay them with as much as 40 % interest. My gambling got so bad, Connie moved back home with her family. This happened about four times during our first few years of marriage. The loan sharks and the drugs were eating up my finances.

One day Connie called and I agreed to meet her for lunch. During lunch we talked about our future together. She wanted a divorce or a commitment from me to be the husband and father she needed to raise our boys. My life was drifting back into the drug scene, but she was not aware of that. She told me how the city had initiated a program for first-time home buyers, and she made arrangements for us to purchase a new home. These were new three bedroom row homes located in the York Town section of Philadelphia.

I'm not sure how she arranged it, but we were approved for a home loan. Shortly after we moved in, she got pregnant and our third son was born. We were a family once again, and all of us were very happy.

My friends and family were amazed at the success of our marriage and the things we had accumulated in spite of my drugs and alcohol problems. We bought a new car, new furniture. All was going well but drugs and alcohol started to come back into my life. My drug friends rode in our new car more than my family.

I started looking for other ways to push my drugs without my wife finding out what I was doing. By this time, I had many different part-time jobs to make extra money, but I maintained my job as a meat cutter and became a Meat Manager for the A&P Stores.

Some of my friends got together and started a social club by the name of *The Incorporators*. We were a group of five guys from different parts of the city who specialized in planning wedding receptions and Cabaret Parties in North and West Philly. I loved when I became a part of this group because it created another outlet with good contacts for me to sell drugs and bootleg whiskey. Also, the opportunity to have affairs with other women was an open field. But that caused my wife and me to have more problems in our marriage.

Later I got involved with a young music group, named, the *Stylistics*. They were a local male rock and roll group from North Philadelphia. It was six of them, three musicians and three singers. They were good entertainers with a good routine. They didn't have a manager, so I convinced them that my group could help them make money by booking them in some of our shows. I became their manager, and I would book them at wedding receptions and local night clubs in Philadelphia and New Jersey. They became a big hit when I started booking them playing for the college parties at Temple and University of Pennsylvania. The money was rolling in again, and my drug sales and use were on the rise. Those college kids had money to burn, and I took full advantage of every opportunity. However, it put a strain on my marriage because I was spending a lot of time away from home, and my wife was getting frustrated.

Also the *Stylistics* were getting frustrated with me. They wanted to become recording stars. But I was more interested in using them as an open door to the college campus to sell drugs and fraternize with the college girls. After all, I was making more money selling drugs than I was with them or with *The Incorporators*, but they didn't know that.

One night the group came over to my house for rehearsal, but the conversation got heated concerning the attitude of my style of management. They expressed their discontent concerning the path that I was taking toward their future. Clarence (C), his brother Doc (Baby Frank) along with Bernard (Lump) became more vocal than the other three. After they

let off some steam and quieted down, I asked for a
few more weeks to seek a recording contract with a
local recording studio. They agreed to give me a little
more time. However, that was short-lived because my
drug problems were taking control. By this time C had
gotten married to the sister of my friend James, and he
managed to help keep my job a while longer.

My wife was sick of my drug habits because by
now I began bringing it into our house. Sometimes
a knock would come at the door late at night. On
a few occasions, the knock came from the police.
They would take me down to the round house (jail) to
question me about some of the big drug deals that
were going on in the city. My wife would cry as they
led me out of the house while my boys watched in a
state of confusion.

One night she lost it when two ladies came to the
house at 3 a.m. looking to buy drugs. That was the
final straw that broke the camel's back. She packed up
right then and moved out, taking the boys with her. It
was cold that night. She wrapped the boys in blankets,
called a cab, and went to her mother's house.

After she left, I turned my house into a speakeasy. I
began selling whiskey, beer, wine, drugs, and anything
else that money could buy. I even rented my boys'
rooms by the hour for sex. My house became a transit
rooming house. If the price were right, I would even
rent my king-size room out for sexual activities.

My house became a repeat of the home environment
that I grew up in. People were coming and going all
night, and my neighbors were not very happy. They
turned me into the police. I had to pay some big fines
for disturbing the peace and later they closed the
place down. There I was in this big house all alone,

devastated from my losses, and feeling very lonely and empty.

Word had gotten back to my wife, and the program under which we purchased the house was the same program that was about to cause us to lose it. She stopped over one evening after work and we talked. She laid out a plan where we could get back together and keep our home. She outlined it like this: **A**-Quit the groups, **B**-Stop the house calls with drugs, **C**-Spend more time with her and the kids, **D**-Get a second job to catch up on bills and save money for Christmas Shopping. I thought that was very reasonable, so I agreed to all she asked and we became a family once again.

We worked hard that year to save money to get out
of debt and to give our boys a big Christmas. I did
everything she asked, but I still struggled with using
drugs and playing poker on the side. She started going
to church, and she accepted Jesus Christ as her Lord
and Savior.

Every Sunday she and the boys went to church. She tried to get me to join them, but I refused. That was my time to get high in my own house without any harassment.

Everything we planned earlier that year was going well and progressing as planned until we got into the Christmas Season.

About two weeks before Christmas, we made plans to start our Christmas shopping, and I was supposed to withdraw the money from PSFS and meet her downtown after work to buy the kids' Christmas items. We even had money set aside for us to buy each other a nice gift. This is something we hadn't done for a few years because much of the time we were separated during the Christmas Season.

I got off work earlier than expected that day so I had some time to kill. It seemed like a good idea to stop by my friend's house to have a holiday drink with him. When I walked into his house, they were partying, gambling, and the drugs were everywhere. I had a few drinks and started gambling. The place got raided by the police, and everyone in the house went to jail.

Here I was sitting in jail, and my wife was standing on the corner in downtown Philadelphia, waiting for me to go Christmas shopping for our kids. What a bummer!!

I waited a few hours for her to get home, and then I gave her a call. I didn't know how to make this into a lie, so I told her the truth. A few hours later, her attorney came down to get me out of jail; but first, he said he had some papers for me to sign. They were my divorce papers along with a paper deeding my portion of the house over to her. I got into an argument with him, but he replied "This is the only way Connie is going to agree to pay your fine." There was another paper he wanted me to sign, a restraining order to leave her and the boys alone and leave the city of Philadelphia. After he made that statement, I was speechless.

I SAT DOWN ON THAT COLD JAIL-HOUSE FLOOR HOLDING MY HEAD IN MY HAND. THAT WAS THE DARKEST MOMENT IN MY LIFE. I KNEW AT THAT MOMENT MY SIX-YEAR MARRAGE TO CONNIE MARIE WAS OVER!!

After I walked out of that jail, I didn't have any place to go. I had burned my bridges with my mother because of an argument we had over money, and she had put me out a few weeks earlier and told me not to come back. I couldn't go to my sister's house because of a fight that I had with her husband over a drug deal. I couldn't stay with any of my friends because I had double-crossed them because of bad drug deals or money.

There I was standing on the cold streets of Philly in front of the round house with everything I owned on my back. I was a free man from jail, but I had no place to go or stay.

A few minutes later another man came out of the jail. He grabbed a yellow cab, and asked the cabbie to take him to the airport. I asked if I could share the ride.

STILL LOOKING FOR LOVE IN ALL THE WRONG PLACES

When we arrived at the airport, I was lost because it was the first time that I had ever been inside an airport and my first time on an airplane. This whole airport experience was new to me. I walked up to the ticket counter and laid fifty dollars on the counter. I asked for the first flight going anywhere leaving Philly. The ticket agent acknowledged that a flight was loading going to Detroit, Michigan.

When I landed in Detroit, it was cold and snowing and the only clothes I owned were on my back, not suitable for a Detroit winter. I didn't have a job, had very little money, no friends or anyplace to stay, so, I hung around the airport wondering what I was going to do. After a while, I met another young man in the airport who looked as though he was also down on his luck. We talked for a while about our current situation and decided to get a cab and go downtown to one of the homeless shelters.

When we arrived downtown, the lines at the shelter were very long. I gave the girl at the front of the line $5 for her spot, and she gladly accepted my offer. Then she jumped out of line and went to the back.

That night I got a hot meal and a warm place to sleep.

During the upcoming weeks while I was living in the shelter, there was a big winter storm that hit the city of Detroit and everyone had to stay put. No one could move during that time. It didn't bother me because I didn't have any place to go or anyone to see. The only thing that I didn't like about being closed in was I had to attend the group meetings, help clean, cook and serve dinner in exchange for staying there.

There was a lady working at the shelter by the name of Mary. She was a counselor who volunteered her time to help the homeless rehabilitate themselves back into the work place. Mary and I became close during my weeks in the shelter and later we developed a relationship. She helped me get a job as a meat cutter at the local food store.

Shortly after I started working, she helped me find my first apartment and the local shelter gave me some furniture. It seemed that my life was going in the right direction once again, but my heart continued to feel empty. I was missing my boys who were back in Philly, but I knew I couldn't do anything about it because of the restraining order Connie had against me. So I bore my feelings and moved ahead to adjust to my new lifestyle.

Mary told me she would continue to work with me only if I didn't get involved in the drug scene, and I agreed. Our relationship continued to grow, and we even made plans to get married after she finished with her degree. I went to her house and met her family, and they welcomed me with open arms. After about a year, Mary got pregnant, and we had a little girl. We were so excited, but we didn't have the finances to get married or to start a family so she stayed at home with her parents while she continued her education. We would get together on my days off and talk about our plans for the future, but it all came down to money. I wasn't sure if I were ready to settle down and get married because my love for drugs had re-entered my life once again, and I wasn't ready to give them up. However, I went along with everything she wanted to do because she was a very good mother to our little girl.

My career with this food chain was moving ahead and that's when I met Tom F. Tom was from West Virginia. This guy was an Elvis look-alike from head to toe. Tom worked for a company that was based out of Grand Prairie, Texas, and he was one of their cattle buyers.

Tom and I hit it off from the start, and we would hang out together whenever he was in town. Tom recognized that I had a good knowledge of the meat business, in retail and in wholesale. He offered me a job as a cattle buyer, and he wanted me to enter their training program. The pay was good, and the opportunity to travel throughout the Midwest was exciting to me. We teamed up, and after traveling with Tom for a few weeks of training, I was on my own. My life was back on track, and it was exciting because it gave me other outlets to sell drugs as I traveled buying cattle from the farmers. The farm hands along with the sons and daughters of the farmers were great customers. They had plenty of money, and I didn't feel bad about taking it. Whenever I came to town to buy cattle, we sold some. The word got around quickly about me and what I was selling. I managed to stay clean with the law.

All of this traveling took a toll on Mary's and my relationship back in Detroit. She continued to push the idea of getting married, settling down and raising a family, but I would sidetrack her comments by changing the subject. Our little girl (Tonya) was approaching two years old. She was very beautiful, and she was the apple of her daddy's eye. On one occasion, Mary and Tonya took a flight and met me in Kansas City, Missouri, where we stayed at the company's apartment for about a week.

Mary had an opportunity to meet some of my co-workers and my new friends. I could tell by her comments that she was not ready for my new lifestyle. I was dressing differently with my western look, cowboy boots, jeans, hat and all. One night we went to a country and western night club, but the music, the crowd, the drinking, and the noise was too much for her to deal with so we left.

After we got in the car, she explained how my new lifestyle was too much of an adjustment for her. She asked me to come back to Detroit with her and Tonya. It took me a while before giving her an answer.

Later that night she told me how much I had changed and I had become a stranger to her. When she left Kansas City that weekend, it was the last time that we ever saw each other again.

There were many times that I wondered what happened to her. I often wondered how my little girl was doing in school, and what type of man she married, how many kids she had. I wondered what her mother told her about her father. What did she say about the man who walked out of her life when she was only two years old? I forgot about my little Tonya, but God said He wouldn't.

Isaiah: 49:15: Can a mother forget about the baby at her breast and have no compassion on the child she has borne though she/he may forget, I will not forget you.

THANK YOU, LORD, FOR NOT FORGETTING ABOUT MY LITTLE GIRL WHEREVER SHE MAY BE!!

A NEW LIFE, PERSONAL AND CAREER WISE

My area of responsibilities had expanded to include Illinois, Indiana, Missouri, Kansas City, Kansas, Iowa, and Nebraska. I was doing very well in my career, as well as with my drugs. I had learned not to let my drug habits interfere with my career, so I worked as hard as I could during the daylight hours and partied with my friends just as hard during the evening. Oh what parties we had!!

One day while I was opening a new store in Gary, Indiana, for the company, I met another buyer by the name of Wayne. Wayne had just closed a meat outlet in Danbury, Connecticut, and he was on his way back to his home town of Union, Missouri, when he stopped by.

Wayne was a slow talking, long-haired, hippie, country boy from a small town in Missouri. We hit it off right away. Both of us loved to get high. We became the best of friends, and he was the best man in my second marriage.

My life was exciting, but the emptiness was still there. When I would be with my friends having fun, I felt as if I were still doing the wrong thing.

I had a lady friend by the name of Becky who traveled with me, but my life still felt empty. I indulged deeper into drugs. Becky and I made a great salt and pepper team especially when we hit the dance floor in those country western joints.

The Lord has made it clear to me why I'm not dead as I look back on the times I spent in those Country Western bar rooms.

Now Becky and I had started drinking tequila straight with a lemon chaser. We picked up these habits while hanging out in those country and western bars back in Kansas City. They would do crazy things like gather a crowd around your table and see who could drink the most tequila. Take a drink and lick the salt off the back of your hand until one of you passed out. One night I got into one of the tequila drinking contests while Becky and some of her friends cheered me on. I put those guys out of commission. Two of them passed out before I did. I suppose the corned whiskey that I grew up drinking prepared me for that moment. I can tell you, I hung with the best drinking that stuff. It also drew the women to me, cowboy boots and all. That's where I met a cowboy by the name of Jack Kennedy.

Jack became another member of our team. He was a good meat man who knew the business like the back of his hand. Jack was married and had three children, but he was unhappy in his marriage, and he didn't hide it. One night when we were hanging out in the company's apartment, I told him about some career opportunities that my company had in St. Louis. I explained how the company was looking for someone with his knowledge who was willing to travel to open some new meat stores.

I'm not sure if it was the weed or the alcohol, but he didn't hesitate, "I'll do it!!" I asked Jack, what about his family? He hung his head and said that he was tired of the family life but didn't know what to do about it because of his kids. He explained that he was already having an affair and stayed away from home most of the time anyway. I didn't get involved with the details of his family relationship because I needed a meat manager for a new store, and he was it.

Wayne, Jack and I were a team that was highly recognized throughout the meat industry for quality, service, and productivity. There were plenty of other companies who tried to entice us with higher wages and benefits. They wanted us to jump ship to join their management team, but we held it together and our company rewarded us for our loyalty. Tom warned us beforehand that this would happen. As soon as we moved into the St Louis area to open three new retail and wholesale meat outlets, the recruiters from other companies were trying to recruit us.

I managed the store on Locus and Hunt Road. Wayne was in South County, Jack was on the Rock Road, and Tom was our overseer. Our personal life was just as good as our career because all of us had similar goals, both personal and career wise.

Loneliness was wearing very heavy on my heart, but I didn't know what to do about it, so I hid it well with drugs and alcohol.

One weekend Wayne and I went to Milwaukee with some friends for the weekend where I met a lovely young lady with a huge afro. Her name was Gloria. We hit it off from the very beginning, and Wayne hit it off with her sister. We told them that we were in town for the weekend in the meat business. Our salt and pepper relationship intrigued them both. They invited us over to their house the following Sunday for dinner. When we arrived, I was impressed with the warm welcome Wayne and I received. It was as if they had known us for years, and I fell in love with the joy of her family atmosphere. They laughed, talked, cooked and enjoyed each other's company without the use of drugs or alcohol. They experienced genuine fun without those things. This was a family atmosphere that I had never seen or experienced before in my life. I fell in love with that life quickly.

The following week I drove back to Racine, Wisconsin, because I wanted to experience that family atmosphere again to see if it were real. I arrived at my hotel late that evening because I wanted to attend Sunday Morning Service with her family. I enjoyed the worship service that morning and I walked out of that church feeling good all over. After church, I was looking forward to my time with Gloria and her family.

Gloria and I dated for only a short time before I asked her to marry me. She was excited and so was her mother because Gloria would be one of the first of her girls to get married. Her sisters were a bit more laid back and told her she should wait a while longer. Her sisters knew of my love for drugs, and I'm sure Gloria had the same knowledge.

We set a wedding date for nine months down the
road, but Gloria kept moving the date up. Thus, we
got married about a month and half after I proposed.
It started small and continued to grow even after
I protested, but she didn't listen to me. When that
day arrived, we got married in her church in Racine,
Wisconsin.

After the wedding, we had our reception in a huge
ballroom not far from the church. I didn't realize she
had so many relatives. My mother came from Philly.
My best man and longtime friend James and his wife
were there. Wayne, another one of my longtime friends
and best man was there also, along with most of
my co-workers from Indiana and Chicago. Everyone
really enjoyed themselves. We left early and drove to
Wisconsin Dells to spend our honeymoon.

That following week I helped Gloria pack, and she moved to Gary, Indiana, where I had rented us a nice furnished three bedroom house. She fell in love with the place when she moved in. She had big plans on changing things around and talked about all the good times we were going to share together, but for some reason I wasn't feeling good about all she wanted to do. After about three months, she got pregnant with our son Mark. This caught me totally off guard because I had made plans to move to St. Louis. We got into a heated argument over leaving the area because she was close to her family. I was already getting bored with our marriage because it wasn't going the way I thought it would. All of those family gatherings that I had enjoyed were not happening any more. All of a sudden it was just Gloria and me, home all alone. We stopped with the laughter and talking like before and I really disliked coming home. Times like this made it easy for me to relate to what my friend Jack was experiencing in his marriage a few years earlier.

One night when I came home, Gloria was lying across the bed crying. I asked what was wrong. She replied; "I feel very lonely, I miss my family, Sunday is my mother's birthday, and you don't show any love and affection toward me anymore."

I took full advantage of her statement by encouraging her to visit her family and spend some time with her mother. I told her that I would take some time off from work and join her in a few a days. At that very moment, she brightened up and gave me a big hug!

When I dropped her off at the bus station the following morning, I knew in my heart that I was not going to Racine to spend time with her and her family.

A year passed and she had given birth to our son Mark, and I wasn't around to be the father and husband she needed for support. I was still chasing my own selfish desires by moving back to St. Louis and hooking up with my old love, Becky. She had put on a few pounds but still looked good. Our stay together was short lived. We parted as friends after a few months together.

Now Mark was approaching two years old, and Gloria was calling everyone she knew who might know where I was living, but nobody gave her any information. One day my sister called and pleaded with me to give her a call. She said Mark was sick and Gloria needed help with medication. At her request, I called.

Gloria and I talked for a long time about what was going on in each of our lives, and we decided to give our marriage another chance.

Gloria and Mark moved to St Louis, where I had a nice two bedroom apartment on the 26th floor of the Mansion House in downtown. We lived together for only about six months before my drug habits kicked back in, and it was more than she could bear. She was disgusted with me and my friends along with our drugs and alcoholic lifestyle. She told me this is not the environment where she was going to raise our son. She walked out of my life. It wasn't until thirteen years later that I saw her and Mark again.

One day I was inspecting a load of meat at the Locus and Hunt Store in West County, St. Louis, Missouri. I met John Colman. John was an executive who worked for "Ralston Purina." John and I talked while his wife shopped and I continued to inspect the meat. He asked if I were the owner and I replied "HELL NO!" I told him jokingly that I didn't have the capital to open an outlet of this nature.

We continued to talk about my background, and he asked "If you had the capital, how would you invest it to open your own business?" I didn't hesitate to give him an answer. I gave him an overview of how I would invest the money. He then identified himself and explained his job function at R.P. He went on to explain that his company had initiated a program to help small business men and women to open their own business in the community. He had my full attention. He asked me to put together a business plan if I was interested, and then give him a call.

It took me about three days to find a location and put my plan together. After I got everything put together, I went to his office in downtown St. Louis to meet with him and other Ralston Purina Executives.

I gave all the executives, who were attending the meeting, a copy of my business plan. It took only about an hour for me to answer their questions. I explained in great detail how my business plan would come together and how I would repay the loan if my plan were approved. I could tell by their expression that they were more impressed with the contents of the package than with the details of the plan.

The wife of a friend of mine dressed the business plan up to look very professional, and I spent time rehearsing my presentation beforehand. It took their board of directors a very short time to approve my $7,000 business loan

above is the newest addition to the Collinsville Beef Company. The new addition comprises 2400 sq. feet of sp

After the loan was approved, I went to work quickly. Wayne and Jack left their place of employment and joined forces with me to open a retail meat outlet in Collinsville, Illinois. The name of my new company was COLLINSVILLE BEEF CO. We did most of the work ourselves, getting the store ready for the grand opening.

Wayne assembled the meat in coolers, Jack took care of the retail end of the business, and I focused on the hiring and the administrative piece of the business. I hired Charlotte as our office manager. She was a long blond-haired blue-eyed country girl with a great personality. It only took us twelve days from the time we started until Grand Opening Day.

(NOTE: I REMEMBER MY AUNT TELLING ME YEARS AGO; WHENEVER I NEEDED HELP, COMMIT THE SITUATION TO THE LORD, AND THAT'S EXCITLY WHAT I DID FOR THIS BUSINESS VENTURE.)

Proverbs 16:3: Commit to the Lord whatever you do and your plans will succeed.

Local businessman expands rapidly in first eight months

REPAYING HIS $7,000 in less than eight months, Leroy Cannady, owner of Collinsville Beef Company, presents John Coleman, Manager of URBAN Affairs for Ralston Purina Company, with a check to cover the money which Ralston put up last fall to enable Cannady to start his meat business. He maintains that a black man's chances in business are "out of sight, provided you have done your homework."

Our Grand Opening exceeded our sales expectations. We were running low on inventory early that afternoon, but our supplier, Snider Packing, reacted quickly with a midnight delivery. This was more business than Snider had anticipated, so we added Royal Packing as one of our suppliers. We thought business would slow down after the grand opening, but our sales continued to go through the roof. We had a staff of six meat cutters, four meat wrappers along with Wayne, Jack, Charlotte, and me. There was such excitement, it seemed as if we couldn't do anything wrong. We made the headlines in the East St. Louis newspapers along with the evening news. This was a big success story for Ralston Purina! Their Public Relations Department made sure the message got out to the media.

We were getting so much business that I repaid my loan to Ralston Purina in record time. This was a big event, and it also made the headlines. Our success attracted other small businessmen and women, because everyone wanted to know the secret of our success.

That's when I met Tim and Rudy. These guys are very hard to describe, but we became bosom buddies. Here I was sandwiched in the group with Jack, Tim, Wayne, and Rudy. Every place we went together, I stood out like a fly in a bowl of milk.

Tim convinced me to get a new car. He had friends who could get anything you wanted at a very good price. I bought a car, a Harley, and a new boat. Man! This is what I call living the good life! I had all the material things anyone could ask for, but deep down inside, I was not happy, and I couldn't understand why.

I decided to take a vacation so I took off to visit my lifetime friend JJ who was living in Buffalo, N.Y. I took the shortcut by going through Toronto, Ontario. I went alone because I needed time to think and try to understand why I was always feeling so empty and lonely.

I enjoyed the ride in my new car. I had the eight track turned up, and I was jamming as I crossed over into Winsor, Ontario. When I arrived in Toronto, I was tired, so I decided to get a hotel room for the evening.

Toronto is a big beautiful city with excitement all around. It reminded me of NYC. I met a young man by the name of Errol, who was from Jamaica. I asked him where I could get a good Canadian meal and a few drinks.

He picked up on the fact that I was from the States and asked if I were driving. If so, he would show me around. When he got into the car, I could tell he wasn't used to nice things. He was jumping and looking around like a kid in a candy factory. We drove down Young Street. I thought he was looking for a place to eat; but he was hanging out the window yelling, trying to pick up women.

We stopped at the light on the corner of College and Young, and the next thing I knew, we had a car full of women he picked up. I enjoyed my stay in Toronto that weekend, and Errol and I became very good friends. In a few days I continued my journey to Buffalo, but I didn't resolve anything concerning the emptiness in my life.

LIFE IS MOVING TOO FAST

When I got back to Illinois, my team and I became even more like family. We were very close. After work everyone would come over to my Mansion House apartment. Sometimes there would be as many as fifteen people sitting around eating, drinking, and getting high. The ladies were impressed with my lifestyle so that opened the door for other off-duty activities.

I wanted to date Charlotte, but she wasn't attracted to my lifestyle and smooth talk. Besides, she had made it very clear to me earlier that she didn't believe in interracial relationships. That didn't stop me from trying to convince her otherwise. She continued to hang out at my place with the rest of the group.

The business was still going strong, and everyone was encouraging me to open another meat outlet in Decatur, Illinois. Jack said he was willing to relocate to get it started. After he said that, it became a done deal. So we opened a second store, and we had the same success as the first one. Soon we opened another one in Wood River, Illinois, and another one in Peoria, Illinois! Wow, business was great! Everyone was happy and prospering financially and materially.

Holiday season was approaching, so I decided to have a big party at my apartment, located in downtown St. Louis, Missouri, for my associates to celebrate our success during the year. My place was packed; the food, the drugs and whiskey were flowing like wild fire. Earlier that day, I had a talk with Tim about my lonely and empty feelings. He smiled and said "It is the drugs that have taken control of your mind."

My choice of drugs was cocaine (white powder) and weed. I smoked weed like most people smoked cigarettes. Sometimes I would toot so much cocaine that my nose would bleed. However, this night I was willing to try something new. One of the ladies at the party turned me on to blotted acid. It was some strange looking stuff. It was a drop of something on a piece of white paper. With my mental state, I was ready and willing to try anything.

I remember trying something like this back in the day when I was at the rock concert at Woodstock in upstate New York. I remember the mind trip I was on that afternoon. I was sitting under a tree listening to the sounds of Janis and anticipating the arrival of Jimmy. Then shortly after I took my first hit of acid, I remembered it made me feel great. I really got into the music, but that stuff messes with your mind. It started drizzling rain. I started freaking out. I was rolling on the ground screaming. I thought there was someone in the tree having bowel movements on me. What a trip! Later I learned that blotted acid was a hallucinating drug.

That night I took a hit of acid, smoked some weed, and had a few drinks. Afterward I was feeling the best that I had felt in a long time.

Everyone was high and were enjoying themselves; even Charlotte.

That was the night Charlotte's wall of restriction concerning interracial dating came tumbling down, and we began dating.

Later that evening some strange thoughts were racing
through my mind at 100 mph. I began hallucinating
as a result of an acid trip, so I walked out on the
balcony to get some fresh air. It was a beautiful night;
the stars were out, and the lights from the downtown
buildings made a wonderful statement. I felt free as
a bird as I looked down across the city of St Louis. I
felt like a bird that had just spread his wings to fly for
the first time. My inner-man had me convinced that
I could fly. I was convinced that I could jump off that
balcony and float lightly down to the streets. I thought
to myself, "Yea, I can do this!" Just as I was about to
climb onto the balcony and jump from the 26th floor
and float through the air, someone pulled my shirt from

behind and shouted "WHAT DO YOU THINK YOU'RE DOING! ARE YOU TRYING TO KILL YOURSELF?" It was Charlotte. She grabbed my shirt and pulled me down from that balcony. Then she held me tightly in her arms. She began crying and told everyone to get out, NOW!

I don't remember all the things she said, but they didn't waste any time leaving. That was the first time Charlotte had shown any feelings toward me.

It was about 3 a.m. when I came to my right state of mind. I looked around and there were Rudy, Tim, and Wayne passed out on the floor with their girls. Everyone else had left.

I grabbed a bottle of wine, rolled me a joint, and sat on the side of my bed looking out the big picture windows overlooking the Mississippi River.

I started thinking about the success of the business we had during the year and the reason for this big celebration. I thought it was me who made it happen. I had reached the top during this business year. I looked around the room and stared at my friends who were passed out on the floor. I replayed in my mind the role each of them had played toward my success. I was very grateful to all of them, and I made a toast to myself on their behalf.

I made another statement that night as I retraced the steps of my journey of building this $500,000 business. I can remember the words that I spoke that night as if I had spoken them yesterday:

"LORD, YOU HAVE TRULY BLESSED ME, BUT I CAN HANDLE EVERYTHING FROM THIS POINT BY MYSELF!!"

Following my big speech, I held up my bottle of whiskey and gave the Lord a toast. At this time I was not aware of the scripture from **Proverbs 16:9 that states, "In his Heart a man plans his course, but the Lord determines his steps."**

After I said that, I fell back across the bed and went to sleep.

The party was over, and it was time to get back to work. We had a big sales season ahead of us, and we had to make plans in order to capitalize on every sales opportunity. I made sure the entire holiday sale items were in the newspapers and scheduled all of them to run on the same day for all the stores. The plans were made, staff was in place, and each store had increased its inventory to handle the big holiday customer flow.

All the ads broke in the daily papers on the same day, but the phone wasn't ringing for orders like it was before. Customers weren't rushing into the stores like before. Everyone was asking, "WHAT'S HAPPENING?"

December turned out to be the worst month we had in my three years in business. I couldn't explain what happened to that 50% sales increase we planned on and anticipated. December was a "do or die" month for most retailers.

We made it through the holiday, but December was the worst month of the entire year. During January our sales continued to decline, and by the end of April, I had gotten so deep in debt with my suppliers, they put me on C.O.D (cash on delivery). I had to close two stores to keep the other stores afloat.

One night my Aunt Alberta called and told me my

mother was sick and she was rushed to the hospital. I didn't waste any time driving home to Philly. I asked Wayne to keep me in the loop on our sales, and if he had to, close the Wood River store to save on expenses. We had massive layoffs during that time.

When I arrived in Philly, my sister and I rushed to the hospital to visit Sal (mom). She had lost so much weight since the last time I had seen her a year ago, she didn't look like herself. She could barely speak. We gave her a big hug and sat with her for the evening. I asked my sister Ann what happened. She told me how much Sal had been drinking over the last year. Her bootleg whiskey business had declined so sharply she couldn't pay her bills, so Ann and her kids moved in to help her out financially.

My mother never returned home from the hospital. She died within two days after I got home. Sal was only forty-eight years old, but she looked like she was seventy.

There was a lot going on in my life during that time: my mother had died, and my business was crumbling. It seemed as if my whole world were falling apart. After the funeral, everyone went to my Aunt's house for some family time together. I saw a lot of my relatives whom I hadn't seen for years. My first cousin Robert was there with his new wife and all five of his sisters. My younger cousin Larry was there with some of his friends.

Larry and I went outside to smoke a joint, and he told me he was dealing drugs in school for some big boys in South Philly. He went on to tell me how much money he was making. I gave him some shortcuts on how to make even more, but I told him that he had to cut corners a little bit. Larry loved my idea and said he would follow through on my advice with his next transactions. Two weeks after Larry and I had that discussion about making more money selling drugs, I received a call from my Aunt Alberta. She told me Larry's body was found in a construction site in South Philadelphia. I cried and thought "Could it have been my advice that most likely cost Larry his life?"

I buried my head in my hand and yelled out to God, "YOU DID THIS! YOU LET THIS HAPPEN!!"

I told my aunt that I will never, never, never step foot in a church again. My aunt tried to comfort me, but I didn't want her prayers. She told me she would continue to pray for me because God had a plan for my life. That was the last time I talked to Aunt Alberta before she died from lung cancer.

When I got back to Illinois, the sales in my stores had gotten so bad I had to close two stores. After that happened, I was too ashamed to face my friends or coworkers. Some of them wanted to come over, but I wouldn't let anyone visit except Charlotte. She was the only person who didn't beat me over the head about all the things I did wrong, and she didn't ask a lot of questions about what happened. The pain was so bad, I drowned myself in alcohol.

I would sit around and cry about what had happened to Larry and the success that I had enjoyed for the last few years. The banks had repossessed my car, my boat, my Harley. They were all gone. I was given five days to move out of my apartment at the Mansion House. After all, I was only $3,500 behind in rent.

I didn't know what I was going to do, so I called my friend Errol and asked if I could move to Toronto and stay with him for a while. He gladly agreed. The next day I caught up with Tim, and he helped me get a used car from a dealer. The good thing about having Tim around was that he could get a person anything he needed anytime, but I skipped town without making one payment on that car.

Everything was moving so fast in my life. I started running from myself. I didn't even tell Charlotte that I was leaving town. She didn't know of my exit plans, and I asked Tim not to say anything to her about my moving to Canada. I left without saying good-bye to her or anyone else. I just wanted to leave Illinois without having to explain to anyone about my failures or future plans because I really didn't have any.

As I was driving through Michigan, heading toward Toronto, I stopped at a rest stop. I was still trying to collect my thoughts and put things together about what had happened to my business in such a short period of time. However, I wasn't coming up with any answers.

Just then a church van filled with young men pulled up beside me. They had a sign posted in the rear window that read:

Proverbs 3: 5-6 : "Trust in the Lord always and do not lean on your own understandings; in all your ways acknowledge Him, and He will make your path straight."

THAT'S WHEN IT HIT ME RIGHT BETWEEN THE EYES! THE WORDS THAT CAME FROM MY MOUTH A FEW MONTHS AGO WERE JUST THE OPPOSITE.

When I said that, "Lord, you have truly blessed me, but I can handle everything from this point by myself!!!" That meant I didn't trust Him anymore.

I sat at that rest stop for hours replaying every step of my downfall after those words came from my mouth on the night I was celebrating my success only a few months earlier.

Now here I was: broke, no job, and no real place to call home, all because I had turned my back on the same God who had blessed me in the beginning. My friend Errol was the only one I could count on at that time.

PROVERBS 19:3 - A MAN'S OWN FOLLY RUINS HIS LIFE, YET HIS HEART RAGES AGAINST THE LORD.

STARTING OVER—BUSINESS AND PERSONAL

When I arrived in Toronto, Errol welcomed me with open arms. He had an apartment only a few blocks off Young Street, but his rent was out of this world. His roommate had moved out the month before, putting him almost two months behind. I told him that I would get a job cutting meat and help with the expenses. Errol did not do drugs, but he drank. It didn't bother him when I did drugs, so we would sit up most of the night drinking wine and talking about our plans for the future. Both of us were excited because this was a new chapter in our lives.

It didn't take me long to get a job, but everyone in the store thought that I was another "draft dodger" from the States. I understood why. Draft dodgers were all over Toronto because they were trying to escape the draft so they wouldn't have to serve in the Vietnam War.

I started working for one of the local chain stores in Toronto where I met Paul. Paul and I became good friends, and he invited me over for dinner. We talked about our goals, and I shared in detail about my past, including my family, personal, and business life. His wife was intrigued. She could not believe that I had done so much in my life in such a short period of time. She asked a lot of questions, and so did Paul. They wanted to know about my drug problems. I convinced them that I was clean, but that was a lie.

One evening Paul and I stopped at a local pub to have a few drinks after work. It was a quiet place in the village. He caught me by surprise when he started talking about moving to the States and opening his own meat business. He asked if I were willing to join him as a partner. I was very thankful, but I told him that I was flat broke! He smiled and said that he had the money, but he wanted me as a partner because I had the skills and knowledge to make it happen.

WOW! Paul gave me a lot to think about that evening, and there was nothing like a joint to sort things out. The thought of returning to the States and starting over from scratch in the small town of Battle Creek, Michigan, was a bit frightening to me at first.

It took a few days, but I agreed to partner with him. I went to his house again for dinner, and later that evening, we started putting together our business plan. His wife Joann was an accountant, but she didn't want to be involved in the daily operation of the business; however, she agreed to file our quarterly reports. She reviewed our business plan, made some corrections, and gave us the go-ahead.

Paul and I took some time off from work, drove to Battle Creek, Michigan, to find a location. Paul and Joann wanted to locate in Battle Creek because Joann's parents lived nearby, and they wanted their boys to be close to their grandparents.

It only took us a few days to find a location and set up a bank account and a line of credit with the newspaper and a few suppliers. I agreed to stay put in Battle Creek while he made plans to relocate his family. I rented a two bedroom mobile home a short distance from the store.

I called my friends Rudy and Tim and asked them to join me in this new venture, and they agreed. They moved in, and we went to work installing the meat coolers and cases. I thought if sales came in as we projected, we would need a few more workers. So I ran an ad and I hired Rex. Later we learned that Rex was the godfather for drugs in the city, but he was still a good meat man and became a good friend.

During the evening times when we were together, Tim, Rudy and I fell back into our old mode of living. Work hard during the day and party just as hard at night. We hit all the night spots, and Rex introduced us to a few of his underground hangouts. I cannot write about all the details that went on in those places, but it was a lifestyle that we were used to. However, Paul was not aware of my double life, and I knew he wouldn't approve, so I kept him and Joann away from all of this.

By the time Paul returned from Toronto and got his family settled, it was time for our grand opening. P&L PRIME MEATS, INC. (Paul & Leroy) was ready to open for business.

I had become known to the underground world of drugs in Battle Creek, and that crowd became some of my best customers. I was their outlet for buying with their food stamps and cashing their food vouchers at a discount price and big profit for the business. Paul was a Canadian, and he didn't understand the food stamp program, so he let me deal with all those transactions. He fell in love with the sales and profit the stamps created, so everything was legal so far as he was concerned.

During the first few months of our new business, the sales exceeded our expectations, and everyone was happy. Everyone was praising me for how the business was progressing. Paul and Joann wanted me to come over to their house every night. I tried to help them understand that I was a single man and my lifestyle was different from theirs (married with children), so we needed space and time apart from each other.

Everyone in the store was so happy, except me. I continued to feel so lonely, empty, and without purpose, but I didn't know what I could do about it. So I hid it with the drugs and alcohol at night.

One night Tim and I were sitting around the house getting high. We started talking about the past, and he suggested I give Charlotte a call. I was not aware at this time that he was playing the two ends from the middle. He was feeding her information about my activities behind my back.

I was a bit hesitant, but I gave in and called her anyway. We hit it off right away, which was good considering we had not talked to each other for over a year. From that night forward, we talked every night during the upcoming weeks. You could say, we fell in love all over again. One night we were talking about what we wanted for our future. That's when I asked her to marry me and move to Battle Creek to be with me.

She loved the marriage part and said "YES," but she didn't like the part about moving to Battle Creek. That part was out of the question. I explained about the business and the income, but she didn't care about any of that stuff. All she wanted was the two of us to start from zero and build our lives together.

She said, "That means the good times, the bad times, and all the times, together!" She reminded me of my past, and said, "Leroy, this is not the type of environment I want to live in and raise children."

The only condition that we could get married was for me to move back to Illinois. I sensed that her sister Carolyn kept reminding her of her past experience with me and had Charlotte convinced that I would leave her again. But this time, it would be 1,000 miles away from home. Charlotte was her little sister, and she was very protective of her. Charlotte had never lived outside her hometown of Maryville, Illinois. Carolyn did not want to see her little sister move that far away from home with someone with my background. She had already told Charlotte repeatedly that I was no good for her, and I would cause her disappointment and pain.

Charlotte and Tim were close friends, so I asked Tim to speak up on my behalf, to reassure Charlotte that I had changed and I wasn't using drugs like I was doing back in St. Louis. He did a good job convincing her and reassuring Carolyn that I would take care of her. She agreed to move, but the wedding had to take place in her hometown of Maryville. I thought that was fair, so we set up a budget. The women did all the planning, and I covered the finances.

One weekend Tim and I drove down to Illinois to follow up on the progress of the wedding. I'll never forget Carolyn's words to me when we were alone.

"LEROY, I WANT YOU TO KNOW THAT I DON'T APPROVE OF YOU MARRYING MY SISTER. IF YOU HURT HER IN ANY WAY, I WILL SPEND EVERY DIME I HAVE FOR SOMEONE TO HUNT YOU DOWN AND BLOW YOUR HEAD OFF!"

She smiled and walked away. I knew in my heart that she meant every word that came from her mouth.

After Carolyn and Charlotte worked out all the details of the wedding, I broke the news to Paul and Joann when we got back to Battle Creek. They were very happy, and Joann agreed that marriage was what I needed, especially to someone like Charlotte. She had never met Charlotte, but Tim talked about her all the time when we were all together.

One night I lay in bed thinking, "Here I am, 30 years old, and now I am on my third marriage. Is marriage something I need to fill the void in my life? Can Charlotte do what Connie and Gloria couldn't accomplish? Why do I think she is any different? I don't know how to be a husband or a father. How will I balance my time between my wife and my business????" I needed answers on how to fill this empty space in my life!!

Rudy was the best man in my wedding, and Paula was Charlotte's bridesmaid. All our friends were there. We had a ball. But later I started getting high and passed out. Wayne and Rudy helped me to my room and laid me across the bed.

Everyone else thought it was from the alcohol, but when Charlotte came into the room, she was not very happy seeing me in that condition on our wedding night.

She was talking and her words were *gusting* at 50 mph about something, but all I wanted to do was sleep. However, she got my attention when she poured a bucket of cold water on me and almost drowned me while I was still in my wedding outfit. She got my attention after that. That was the first time that I had ever seen this side of her. She told me, "I DON'T CARE IF YOU ARE HIGH, YOU ARE NOT GOING TO FALL ASLEEP ON ME ON OUR WEDDING NIGHT!!" She was right, and she had her way!

That next morning we went down for breakfast, and she commented, "I wonder what the hotel staff will think when they see one half of the bed soaked in our honeymoon suite."

A NEW LIFE IN A NEW CITY

The drive to Battle Creek was quiet during the first few hours. I could tell that Charlotte was in deep thought. Besides, this was a new chapter in her life. Leaving home for the first time had to be hard.

I didn't want to mislead her by telling her everything was going to be easy. Also, she was downhearted because she had to give up her English sheep dog, Jason, which she had owned ever since he was a puppy. They were very close, and she had to give him up because they didn't allow pets where we were living.

Charlotte's family was small but very close. She had lost her brother in the Vietnam War, and her father had died from cancer a few years earlier. I never met her father, but she told me it was good that I hadn't. She said he would have shot me on site for having a relationship with his daughter. Her natural mother died from colon cancer when Carolyn was a young girl, so it was Charlotte, Carolyn, and her stepmother.

Based on what I learned about her family life, I knew I had to step up and be all that she needed as a husband. She was not accustomed to my lifestyle, so I was the one who had to make the transition to what she needed me to be as a family man.

When we arrived at our new home, we received a warm greeting from Paul and his family. Paul's wife Joann and Charlotte hit it off right from the start.

Charlotte spent the first few days cleaning up our mobile home. She made it look and feel very homey. Rudy and Tim didn't return to Battle Creek, so it was just the two of us living there. Every evening she had dinner on the table when I got home from work. We ate, talked, and laughed about some of the things in our past, but I could tell she wasn't totally happy. Then one day I came home from work early and found her crying. She told me how lonely she was because she missed her family. Even though they talked for hours on the phone every night, it was not the same as being there. She knew everything that was going on in their lives, but she was still homesick. She was also close to her niece and nephew, which made things harder. We had a glass of wine, and after a while, she settled down, and we enjoyed the rest of the evening.

The following day she suggested getting a part-time job to fill in the empty hours in her day. I agreed, and she was excited about that.

Rex and Renee (a department manager at the local K-Mart) started coming over often. Renee and Charlotte became very good friends. They were about the same age, and Renee was what Charlotte needed to help her stay focused on her new lifestyle. Also, Joann was the key to helping her overcome her homesickness.

Renee helped Charlotte get a job at K-Mart as a bookkeeper, and that worked out great. Renee and Rex came over every night to join us for dinner. The four of us became like a family. Rex and I would get high after dinner, while Charlotte and Renee would sip on a glass of wine. Neither one of them got high, but they didn't object when we did. Charlotte was aware of my past history with drugs, but all was good as long as it didn't affect my working relationship with Paul or our marriage. She kept close observations to make sure that I didn't overdo it.

A strange thing happened one day. Charlotte came home from work with a guinea pig....A GUINEA PIG!!

"What's the meaning of this?" I asked. She said K-Mart was closing the live pet department, and they offered the staff an opportunity to purchase the pets at a reduced price, so she got a guinea pig! She named him Charlie.

He was a cute little fellow. Here I was, 30 years old, and this was the first time in my life that I had ever had a pet in the house. I fell in love with the little rat. I would let Charlie run around on the floor when I was home, and he grew big. Charlie got too big for the small cage, so I just let him live and run loose around the house.

I started spending a lot of time with Charlie, and we learned how smart this little fellow was. I taught Charlie how to jump over his toys, roll a ball across the floor, and I even taught him how to swim in the bath tub. He was so amusing! One day Rex and I taught him how to do back flips.

You see, every night when Rex and I got high, Charlie would stand on his hind legs in front of us while we smoked a joint, and I would blow smoke from the weed in his face. After a while, Charlie got high and started running around in circles, which was so funny to all of us. Charlie became a new member at our pot-smoking parties.

The sales in our meat business were still going strong. Paul was very happy, and our relationship was closer than ever.

One day I was hanging out with Rex on my day off when we went to a drug house of one of his friends. When we arrived, the activities at the place reminded me of old times back in St. Louis. I fell in love with that drug atmosphere, and that drug house became a regular stop for me. Charlotte and Paul were not aware that my drug activities had kicked in again, but it wasn't long before Charlotte noticed a change in my behavior.

One day while we were having dinner, she confronted me about my activities, but I lied about the whole thing. I believe she knew I was lying, but she wasn't the kind of person to start an argument without having hard evidence. Her silence did more damage to me than a heated argument.

After a while, Charlotte met some ladies at work, and they invited her to attend a Bible study. I was glad she joined the group because it gave me flexibility to visit the drug house, and I didn't have to account for my time. However, it didn't take long before I was hitting cocaine on a regular basis, and my drug habit got to be very expensive. It was costing me more money than I had left over from my pay check.

In order to support my drug and gambling habits, I stopped paying all the bills at home and started taking money from the business account to support my addictions. I started gambling, and that got me deeper in debt with the loan sharks because I had to borrow money from them to cover my gambling losses.

Paul trusted me to pay the bills and take care of the daily bank deposits for the business. After a while, I got so deep in debt with the loan sharks, I started taking cash from the deposits and using it to support my drug and gambling habits, without anyone noticing it. One day Charlotte got home before I did, and she opened the mail and saw all the past due notices from bill collectors. She asked me about them that evening, and I knew then that I was "busted." She looked deeply into my eyes, and I knew I had to tell her a story that was convincing. She didn't push the issue even after I fed her a line and told her that it was a mistake. I could tell by her attitude for the rest of the evening that my answers didn't satisfy her curiosity. Charlotte came home from Bible study one night after church and told me she had accepted Jesus Christ as her Lord and Savior, and she wanted us to start going to church on Sunday. I told her I was not ready for that, and I didn't want her bugging me about going to church and this Christ stuff

Shortly after this, she, Joann, and Renee started a Bible study in our home, and that put a monkey wrench in my lifestyle. I didn't like those Christians coming into my house. There was one member of the group who would always ask me, "Do you pray?"

I told her, "No," but that my wife did. I was getting fed up with their coming over twice a week. After a while, I lost it! I called Rex and some of our drug friends over for a party on the same night they had their Bible study. I was going to show them that they weren't going to interfere with my lifestyle of getting high in my own house.

Charlotte didn't like my change of attitude toward her Christian friends. She knew something was seriously wrong, and she even confronted me about my drug use. She noticed it had become more than just a social high every night because it had affected our love life also. She would kneel and pray aloud when we went to bed and ask for blessings on our household.

That bugged me even more, so I stopped going to bed at the same time she did. Most of the time, I would pretend that I had paperwork to do, so I waited until she went to sleep before I got into bed. I couldn't stand to hear her praying.

The drugs and gambling had really gotten the best of me. I was in debt to the loan shark for thousands of dollars. When I was gambling at the poker tables, I just couldn't stop - even when I was losing big.

One night I thought I had a winning hand in draw poker (full house, three queens, and two sevens), so I borrowed a few thousand dollars from the loan shark in order to bet my hand. However, he made it very clear to me that he needed his money back within 48 hours.

All the players in the house stopped what they were doing to watch our hands play out. The other two players folded, so it was just Sam and me. I bet 500; he called and raised it a thousand. I really didn't think that he could beat my hand, so I called and raised another 500. He called. You could have heard a pin drop as the crowd watched.

I laid down my full house with a big smile on my face, thinking that I had the winning hand. I told him to "read um and weep!!

Sam laid down his hand; he had four 9s. I WAS SICK, SICK, SICK, SICK! Then out came all these curse words.

The house couldn't believe that someone could be so lucky, and neither could I. Before I left the house that evening, the loan shark reminded me again that he needed his money within 48 hours. I reassured him that I would have his money on time.

I didn't go home that night because I had to find a way to come up with the money. I stayed with Rex, and I told him what had happened at the drug house. He could tell that I was sick and not in my right mind. I paced the floor of his living room, cursing, and smoking one joint after another. All I wanted to do was get high. I thought that would ease my pain.

When I wasn't home by midnight, Charlotte was calling around to find out where I was. She called Renee who told her that Rex and I were passed out on the couch. Renee knew that I was not asleep, but she didn't tell Charlotte that I was in a state of rage.

The following morning I went straight to work early so I could put the weekend deposit together. We had a good weekend in sales and a fair amount of cash and checks. One thing I learned during my years of dealing drugs is that you don't play with a loan shark's money no matter how well you know him! When he gives you a repayment schedule up front, you comply. If not, you put your life in his hands. So I took all the cash from the deposit to repay the loan shark.

Now that I had taken the money from the bank deposit, I had to come up with a plan to put it back. So I started taking money from one day's deposit to balance the deposit for the previous day. This went on for a while, but it caught up with me because sales got slow. I didn't have the cash to balance the previous day's deposit. Checks began to bounce. Payroll checks, expense checks: all of them started bouncing. I didn't know what to do, so I told everyone that our bank had made a big mistake, and I asked them to give me a few hours to get everything straightened out. I left the store.

Now Paul asked his wife Joann to get involved balancing our account because she had an accounting background. I knew she would find out quickly about what I had been doing, and she did. She called my wife and told her what had happened. Charlotte rushed home from work that afternoon, and she found me stretched out on the couch, stoned out of my mind. She pulled me up by my shirt and asked me to explain what had happened. I tried to explain, but I couldn't maintain my train of thought.

She started crying and praying. I told her that her prayers wouldn't do us any good. In my state of mind, I really tried to convince her to steal the money from her company's bank deposit.

I was losing my mind! The loan sharks - the bank deposits - asking her to steal for me! I didn't know what I was going to do.

I felt like running out on the highway in front of a truck and letting someone put my lights out. It seemed as if that was the only way I could have peace in this world.

I got sick of her praying. I yelled and told her to keep quiet and to stop all that prayer stuff!!!

Paul had to close the store early that day because we didn't have the money to buy the inventory to stay open. All the workers refused to return to work until they got their paychecks. Paul and Joann came over to the house to discuss plans as to how I was going to resolve these issues. I was too high to give them any answers. I just didn't have the answers.

Paul looked me straight in the eye with tears rolling down his face and said in a quiet voice, "Leroy, how could you do this to us? We trusted you! I moved my family down here from Canada because I trusted you. How could you do this to my family? Even my children trusted you; how could you do this to them?"

His words cut deeply, but no one tried to understand my circumstances. What about me??

When Paul walked out of my house that afternoon, he was crying hard. After that day, I never saw Paul nor Joann again.

I learned later from Rex that they moved in with Joann's parents in Detroit because they had lost everything. Everything they owned was tied up in the business. They had to pull their three boys out of private school and put them in public schools because they were broke. Going to public schools was the first time in their lives that this had happened.

My action was even too much for Charlotte to handle. She looked at me with an empty expression on her face. She picked up the phone while I was standing there. She called her sister and asked her to come to Battle Creek to get her because she was moving back home. Their conversation was short, and I could tell that Carolyn didn't ask her any questions.

When Carolyn arrived in Battle Creek that Friday morning, I made it a point not to be home. I knew what her attitude would be, and I couldn't face her after what had happened. I spent the early part of the day at Rex's house getting high on cocaine. When I got home later that afternoon, they had packed up and gone.

I looked around the house, and all that homey stuff that made my house so warm and friendly was gone. The pictures of our wedding that covered the wall unit were gone; the handmade bedspread and decorated towels in the kitchen and bathroom were gone. The house felt empty, and there was coldness as if the weather were freezing, but the outside temperature was in the upper 80's.

Even my little friend Charlie was gone. I had gotten used to his whistle when I walked into the house. It was quiet; a silence like I had never experienced before. I pulled out a bottle of whiskey, rolled me a joint, and started drinking straight from the bottle until I passed out.

I was hurting all over. I felt deep pains of loneliness all over my body. I wanted to cry, but tears wouldn't fall, so I screamed, and screamed, and screamed until I couldn't scream anymore.

I remember shaking my fist and looking up at God and yelling, **"YOU DID THIS; YOU CAUSED ALL THIS TO HAPPEN TO ME.... YOU DID IT!!"**

I was hurting so badly, I didn't know whom else to blame.

Getting drunk was the only thing that helped me make it through that night.

II. FINDING REASON

THE DAY I WANTED TO DIE!

The following morning I woke up early. It was a beautiful day, but that coldness was still in my house, and here it was late May. I rolled a joint, tooted some cocaine, and took me two hits of blotted acid. It didn't take long until I was stoned out of my mind. I went for a walk down by the county park in Battle Creek.

On my way to the park that morning, I ran into some of my drug buddies, and they asked if they could come over and get high later. I told them that would be great because I didn't want to be alone. I continued my walk to the park.

When I got to the park that morning, there were homeless people lying around on the ground and on the park benches. It seemed as if everyone was in his own world.

I grabbed a spot on one of the empty benches, and I stared up at the trees and watched everything that was going on around me. I watched the kids throwing stones at the ducks in the small lake. I watched the homeless men sharing drinks from the same bottle, wrapped in a brown paper bag. I watched as two teenagers shared a joint together. Everyone was caught up in his world without having any concerns for anyone or anything going on around him.

I sat there for a while, lost in my thoughts and caught up in my own world of self-pity as I watched their activities. I began to recap my own life: Working in the basement, bottling bootleg whiskey, witnessing the death of my father and spending time in a jail cell for his murder, getting kicked out of the military, the failed relationship with my friend Charlie when I was a teenager, failed marriages with Connie and

Gloria, disappointing times in business, the broken relationship with my trusted friend Paul and his family, and now my third wife had walked out on me.

Those thoughts continued to race through my mind so much so I couldn't stand them anymore. Nothing came to mind of any good that I had done for anyone during my entire life, unless it was for my own selfish gain.

It was on that day when I came to the conclusion that in the world's eye, it would be better off if Leroy Cannady were dead! I tried, but I just couldn't erase those thoughts. I needed peace from the pain of emptiness that had been haunting me all my life.

I couldn't handle it anymore. It was that morning that I decided to go home and start popping pills and take whatever drugs I could find and kill myself. I relished that thought because it seemed like it was the only solution to ease my pain.

I got up from that park bench, stretched, took a deep breath, and then headed toward home to carry out my suicidal plan. I couldn't think of a better way to leave this world than to leave stoned out of my mind on dope. What a way to go!

I started walking toward the house thinking I had put together a good plan to take my life. I knew I could not find the words to explain the emptiness I was feeling on that day, but the thought of taking my own life was very real. I truly believed that this was the best way to ease my pain and to fill the emptiness that had haunted me my whole life. Besides, it would settle all my debts.

I thought it was a good plan. It would be the solution to all my problems in life.

Now there were some well-dressed men in the park that morning. They were talking to the homeless people, and they were giving them some little Testaments (Bibles). One of those men walked up to me with a big smile on his face and said, "DO YOU KNOW JESUS?" I said, "NO, AND I DON'T WANT TO KNOW JESUS!"

He was carrying a handful of those little Testaments, and he had a large Bible tucked under his arm.

That morning I was hurting so badly. I felt so empty, and I knew that my life was so dirty that Jesus was the last name I wanted to hear.

I told him that I didn't want to hear anything about his Jesus!

He said, "JESUS LOVES YOU!" I replied, "If you knew all the things that I have done in my life and all the people whom I've hurt....no one can love me!"

I didn't want to stand there and talk about his Jesus, so I pushed him aside, and all his Bibles fell to the ground.

I reached down to pick up his large Bible, and when I did, my eyes were glued to the page of Isaiah 1:18-19, which said:

"Come now, let us reason together," says the Lord. "Though your sins are like scarlet, they shall be as white as snow; though they are red as crimson, they shall be like wool! If you are willing and obedient, you will eat the best from the land."

Something happened to me at the moment. Those words did surgery on my soul. I tried to look away, but I couldn't take my eyes off that page. Those words were cutting into me deeply. It was as if someone had grabbed my heart and mind and was holding them in his hands.

I began to shake like a leaf on a tree. Then I fell to my knees and began crying. Tears were falling down my face very heavily. I tried to stop, but I couldn't. I was crying out of control. People in the area were staring at me. I heard someone in the crowd say, "He's acting like a mad man." I was so ashamed of myself; I buried my head in my hands.

That man picked up one of those little Testaments. He opened it, and showed me:

John 3:16 : "For God so loved the world that He gave His only begotten Son that whosoever believes in Him shall not perish but have everlasting life."

It was then that I personalized that scripture.

"For God so loved Leroy Cannady that He gave His only begotten Son."

That man showed me other scriptures. He turned to **Roman 10:23: "FOR WHOEVER CALLS ON THE NAME OF THE LORD SHALL BE SAVED."**

I was still crying, but now I knew that it was Jesus whom I needed to heal the hurt and the emptiness in my life.

It was then that this man led me in a prayer, and I prayed and asked Jesus Christ to come into my heart, to forgive me of my sins, to clean up my life, and make me somebody.

I want you to know that the Lord heard my prayer and answered my prayer immediately.

A LIFE THAT WAS CHANGED!

The Lord Jesus healed my broken heart instantly, and I lost my dependence on drugs. At that very moment, I had a cleared head. I was cleaned all over from that emptiness that I had carried around all my life. It was gone! I felt like a new person! I WAS SO EXCITED!!

Everyone around me thought that I really was a mad man. They started moving away from me slowly. I wanted to grab all of them and give them big bear hugs. I felt like a new man!

The Lord heard my prayer that day, and He answered my prayer. I was healed from my addiction instantly. All the hurt, the loneliness, and the void were gone. I felt whole! Complete!

I started home to call my wife to share my life-changing experience with her, but on my way home I ran into my drug friends who were hanging out on the corner. They had asked to come over to my house earlier to get high.

I was glad when I saw them. I began sharing with them about my life-changing experience. They looked at each other, and they replied in a drunken and slurred tone, "You have lost your f*%$ mind! That cocaine and acid have fried your mind!"

They said, "We are not going over to your house if you are going to talk that Jesus stuff to us."

I knew at that moment they were too high for me to make sense to them, so I went home alone.

When I got home, I called Charlotte and shared with her about my life-changing experience. We talked for almost an hour, and she replied, "I can tell something is different about you because we've been talking for almost an hour and you haven't said one curse word."

CAN YOU BELIEVE THAT? THE LORD HAD TAUGHT ME HOW TO SPEAK ENGLISH!

My wife and I got back together after I moved to her hometown of Edwardsville, Illinois. We joined a local church, and we dedicated our marriage to the Lord.

The Lord blessed our marriage. Doctors had told Charlotte that she would never be able to bear children. I remember the day when she came home from the doctor's office and gave me the news. I thought that our plans to have a large family were over, but she grabbed my hand and smiled.

She said, "We are not going to worry about things we can't control. Instead, we are going to trust the words of our Lord and Savior, Jesus Christ!"

Luke 18:27: "Jesus replied, 'What is impossible with men is possible with God.'"

Less than six months later, Charlotte was pregnant with our first daughter Christina Renee.

One year after Christina was born, Charlotte became pregnant with twin girls. We named them AMBER JOY and AUTUMN LYNN. It wasn't until the day of delivery that we discovered the twins were co-joined at the hip. A few weeks later they died.

Charlotte lived in that Maryville Hospital for 47 days with the twins. She was there with our older daughter, Christina, aged two, every day to change every diaper and to wipe away every tear from the twins' eyes. She came home briefly each day but returned. She spent time reading those Bible stories and praying. I watched as she read to them, and I really believe that it gave them peace.

Even Christina at her early age would lie in her mother's arms peacefully as she listened to her mother read Bible stories to her twin sisters.

Matthew 19:14: "Jesus said, 'Let the little children come to me, and do not hinder them, for the Kingdom of heaven belongs to such as these.' "

After Bobby and Michael came another little girl. We gave her the name from each of the twins, AMBER LYNN. We were blessed! The Lord kept His promise to me.

Isaiah 1:19: "If ye are willing and obedient, you shall eat good from the land."

III. LIVING REASON: WITH GOD

I SURRENDER ALL

During our early years of marriage, I still had my struggles with cigarettes and alcohol. I wasn't drinking so much that I would pass out, but on weekends I really tied it on come Friday night. I was smoking two packs of cigarettes a day, and I handled all the finances.

I remember going to church one Wednesday evening, and we had a special speaker. He had a very challenging message. At the end of the service, he asked if anyone had anything in his life that was hindering the walk with the lord.

He said, "Let this song be your prayer: I SURRENDER ALL." He also asked the church to come forward and pray as we sang that song.

People started moving forward toward the altar. I was singing, but I didn't move from my seat. My wife looked at me as if to make a statement for me to go forward, but I still didn't move. She moved closer to me and jabbed me in the side with her elbow. Suddenly I found myself in the aisle with the crowd. I started moving toward the front of the church. When the speaker began to pray, I knelt at the altar for prayer. After the prayer, I got up and returned to my seat. On the way home, Charlotte asked if I were serious about my prayer and the song that I sang. I replied, with a hearty, "YES, I'M SERIOUS!"

I lay awake that night thinking about all the things that were going on in my life. The Lord had totally delivered me from my dependence on drugs, but the cigarettes and alcohol were still a factor. I tried to quit smoking, but I couldn't quit. I had cut back on my drinking, but I still loved the taste and the way the whiskey made me feel after a full day's work.

That following week I asked Charlotte if we could do something different for the weekend because I needed time to get away to clear my thoughts of what was going on in my head. The cigarettes, the alcohol, the prayer: *("I SURRENDER ALL").* All that stuff was getting to me, and I needed time away from church to get myself together. I just had to get away, but I didn't tell Charlotte that.

She suggested we go camping for the weekend. That was fine with me, but camping was something that I had never done before; however camping became a regular event for our family. After all, she was a country girl.

I was thrilled when she taught me how to put the tent up and build a campfire. Can you believe this was fun?? It was a little weird at first: the darkness, the sounds of the outdoors, the fire, the tent as our home, but after I adjusted to the surroundings, I slept like a baby that night. IT WAS SOOOO PEACEFUL!

During this weekend, our marriage began to grow, and we became even closer than man and wife. We became close friends. We laughed; we talked, read our Bible, and sang some of the old-time Christian favorites.

Our singing caught the attention of Glen and Jenifer, with their new baby — another couple that was camped out nearby. They joined us the following evening for food, praise and worship.

After we got back home, Charlotte kept in touch with Glen and Jenifer. We became very good friends, and we spent just about every weekend at each other's houses. Both of the wives recognized that Glen and I were what each other needed for our Christian growth.

Glen and I were both meat cutters, and we started working for the same company (The KROGER Co.) in St. Louis. Soon I was promoted to the position of Meat Manager, and Glen was my lead meat cutter.

Charlotte and I had issues with our finances. It seemed as if my whole pay check were eaten up each week by unexpected expenses. I couldn't pay the bills on time; we fell behind. I mean *way* behind! Part of it was due to my drinking and smoking, a big expense that I made a high priority.

I was getting sick of bill collectors calling me at work about overdue payments, I was sick of not being able to buy a new family car. I was sick of all this church stuff about giving more to the church. All this kind of teaching wasn't getting us anywhere.

I'm sure Charlotte could see the frustration because she stopped talking to me about church things. We even began arguing about finances. We went to church that Sunday and the pastor's message was on faithful giving (tithing), and that made me mad. I was ready to start attending another church.

On the way home, I told Charlotte that all the church wanted was money. She said that we should start tithing. When she said that, I stopped the car. I asked her if she were out of her mind. I went into a state of rage, concerning giving more money to the church. The kids in the back seat started crying which just added to my frustration.

GIVING MORE MONEY TO CHURCH, ARE YOU NUTS????? I lost it that afternoon!

We couldn't make ends meet now, and she wanted to add to it by giving more than my $15.00 a week to the church! That was the amount that I had set aside each week for my giving. It didn't matter that I was making $650.00 a week. That's all that I was going to give to ANY CHURCH!! And I made that very clear!

Later that day when I settled down, I came up with this great plan. I suggested that she handle the finances and maybe she could see how tight our finances were.

She gladly agreed to take over that responsibility. It just blessed my heart to get her off my back about this tithing stuff.

She was not aware that our credit was so bad at the time we couldn't buy a box of corn flakes on credit. But now she could see what I was talking about. I even suggested we start attending the Assemblies of God church in downtown Edwardsville, Ill.

I told her I wanted to attend this church because we didn't know anyone, and I understood they had a good children's ministry. She was not in favor of that idea at all, but after considering my request for a few days, she gave in to my wishes

I thought this was a great way for her to get away from all those ladies in the church who were a bad influence on her. Or so I thought. Changing churches just added to my problems with giving. She didn't waste any time researching the church in downtown Edwardsville. The name of our new church was: Edwardsville AOG Church.

This church had a lot going on for the family, and Charlotte and the kids got involved in everything. The church even had a Sunday night service, something our last church didn't have. I didn't like that too much. It took me a few weeks before I started attending all three services.

She went to work right away with our finances. She said that we were going on a budget, and she needed to know how much money I needed each week for gas, lunch, union dues, cigarettes and alcohol. I gave her a number, and she agreed to work with it.

I smiled and thought to myself: "This is more than what I'm spending already. I am going to love this new approach! I'll bet she'll last about two months, and she'll be begging me to take the check book and start paying the bills again."

That following Sunday I didn't go to church because I knew our pastor was going to be long-winded that morning, and I wanted to watch the opening half of the football game between the Redskins and the Cowboys.

After church my four-year-old daughter Christina ran into the house and jumped up in my lap, gave me a big hug, and said, "Daddy, I prayed to Jesus while I was in Sunday school this morning that you will quit smoking them cigarettes!" (This was the Sunday school class her mother taught.) It was that moment when the smell of those cigarettes in the ash tray made me sick. I picked up the ash tray, walked into the bathroom, and emptied it. I held my little girl's hand and smiled. I told her Jesus had answered her prayer. I took the rest of the cigarettes and flushed them down the toilet.

When I did that, she ran into her mother's room and said with excitement, "MOMMY, MOMMY, DADDY QUIT SMOKING, LOOK, MOMMY, HE PUT THEM IN THE TOILET! MOMMY, JESUS ANSWERED MY PRAYER! HE REALLY DID, MOMMY!!"

1 John 5:14-15: This is the confidence we have in approaching God: that if we ask anything according to his will, he hears us. And if we know that he hears us, whatever we ask, we know that we have what we asked of him.

My wife looked deep into my eyes and said in her soft but firm tone, "I hope you're not playing around with her emotions!"

I had seen that look in her eyes many times in the past, and I knew that she was very serious. I assured her that it was real!!

Friday of the same week the Lord delivered me from alcohol. It was a day when I met up with my friends after work for "HAPPY HOUR!" When I joined them, the bartender had two of my favorite drinks on the bar, but I reached for the glass, and as it got close to my lips, the smell of the scotch made me sick to the stomach. I set it down, waited for a moment, and tried to take a drink, but the smell made me even sicker.

I ran into the restroom, washed my face with cold water, and looked at myself in the mirror as I dried my face. That's when it hit me: "I SURRENDER ALL!" It was that moment, when I realized that the Lord Jesus Christ had also delivered me from my alcohol addiction.

I went back into the barroom, I told my friends that I was going home, and this was the last time that I would meet with them on Friday. They asked why, but I didn't know how to explain to them in more details because they were not Christians.

When I got home that evening, I was greeted at the kitchen door by my little girl. She said, "Daddy, me and mommy was praying that you'll come home early today, and you did! Daddy, I love Jesus!!"

A few months had passed since we had joined the new church, and everything was going well. I loved the preaching of the Word and the style of worship. I had started to get involved with the men's ministry.

One thing I noticed when I was at work: the bill collectors weren't calling and harassing me anymore. This went on for a while and I fell in love with this new-found freedom.

One evening we had some friends over for dinner and afterward we had a time of sharing testimonies. All of them were sharing how the Lord had blessed them in so many ways, and then I began to share in a joking way that I was blessed that bill collectors had stopped calling me at work. I joked and said that the Lord had showed them that I was broke, and it wasn't worth their time to keep calling me.

Everyone laughed, and some responded by saying they needed that kind of blessing. At that point,

Charlotte silenced the crowd by sharing why the bill collectors had stopped calling me at work.

She said, "WE STARTED TITHING, AND THE LORD HAS BLESSED OUR FINANCES!!"

When she said that, my mouth was open, and I was lost for words. I let her finish talking, and I was listening in disbelief to every word that came from her lips. After she finished, another couple spoke up with their testimony, and then another. All the while, I was speechless. I could not wait until everyone left because I had a million questions to ask Charlotte.

I asked her to explain how all of this came together, and she did. She attended a mid-week prayer meeting and asked the Lord to give her wisdom and insight on handling our finances. Her starting point was to have an obedient spirit, and that she had. The second was to contact all our creditors and set up a repayment arraignment to stay current with payments.

One of our creditors was so impressed with what she wanted to do, he suggested that he team with her and combine all our bills. I remember signing the papers, but I didn't think too much about what she was telling me or what I was signing. Listening to what my wife was telling me was a big problem that I had during that time. She told me what she was doing and what I was signing.

Then she went on to explain how she started giving to the Lord and how He had blessed our finances. I could not believe how she had made my pay check go so far.

This made a believer out of me. Not to a point of giving in order to get something in return but a sign of obedience. About a year later I got a promotion with the assistance of the store manager with Kroger and that added to my income. We bought a new car, new furniture, and we were able to take family vacations to places we couldn't afford earlier.

Malachi 3:8-10: Will a man rob God? Yet you rob me. But you ask, 'How do we rob you?' "In tithes and offerings. You are under a curse-- the whole nation of you-- because you are robbing me. Bring the whole tithe into the storehouse, that there may be food in my house. Test me in this," says the Lord Almighty, "and see if I will not throw open the floodgates of heaven and pour out so much blessing that you will not have room enough for it" . . . says the Lord Almighty.

2 Corinthians 9:7: Each man should give what he has decided in his heart to give, not reluctantly or under compulsion, FOR GOD LOVES A CHEERFUL GIVER! AAAAAAMEN!

MOVING FORWARD

God's blessings were flowing far beyond what I ever expected. One night my pastor gave me an invitation to attend a dinner that was sponsored by the Gideons. I thought this was a great opportunity to take my wife out to a nice restaurant, enjoy a great meal, and the best part of all, "It was free!"

At the beginning of the meeting, the moderator opened with prayer, and he made the statement: "You may notice there are no ash trays on the tables, because Gideons don't smoke!" The meal was great, the program was also. At the end of the meeting the challenge was given to the attendees to fill out the application on the table and become a member of the Gideons International.

I noticed men and their wives were filling out the application, but I folded my application and put it in my pocket. A Gideon at our table asked if he could pray with us about joining, I agreed, but I had no intention of joining the Gideons. After he completed his prayer, my wife urged me to fill out the application. She gave me an elbow to the side and a look that led me to believe that it was in my best interest to fill out that application. It was that night that we became members of the Gideons International.

From the very start, my wife became active with the ladies. She attended all the meetings and luncheons, and she took me right along with her everywhere she went on Auxiliary business. It wasn't long until the Lord started moving on my heart, and we began working together as a team with this association of Christian business and professional men.

The Lord continued to pour out His blessing in our family and in my career. I was selected to participate in a new management training program that my company wanted to initiate. They selected 20 Department Managers from over a 1,000 of their stores to participate in the new training program. They flew us to the home office in Cincinnati, Ohio, and spent five days outlining the program and its purpose for the next 18 weeks. The CEO explained how this training would take us away from our families for five days a week. He went on to explain how we would spend that time with special instructions from Parnell, Purdue, Carnell University and Kent School of Law in Chicago. They went on to explain that our training would focus on fine tuning our managerial, people, communication, reciting and training skills and contract negotiations skills with unions. They filled our heads with how we were hand selected because we stood out among our peers in our field of expertise (my background was meat). I can tell you, when we finished that week in Cincinnati, we were walking on water. It was a time when we thought nothing could touch us; our heads were so big, our peers noticed a change when we returned to our division. They even gave our group a name, "The Elites." We had quality T-Shirts with a big letter "E" on the front. We took our first group photo which was distributed throughout the entire company as to who we were and who we represented: THE BEST OF THE BEST!!

After our training concluded, we had the knowledge and skills of a college student who was top in his class in the areas we were trained. We were the best and our newfound knowledge and attitude reflected in our actions. More than half of the men left the company and became CEO at other retail food chain stores. The ones who remained with the company experienced a sky rocket career, and our salaries more than doubled. We were very cocky because we had something that no one else had. We had the knowledge and we only reported to the executive officer in the company. It didn't take them long to realize they had created a management force that exceeded their expectations in every area under our control. But it created a hostile environment among top level Regional and Zone Managers. We had an attitude that we could not do anything wrong.

I remember one executive telling us during his closing speech at our graduation;

"YOU BETTER LOOK OUT FOR THE BOAT WHEN YOU'RE OUT THERE WALKING ON THE WATER!"

In other words, no matter how good you are, you can still fall.

With my new career path and making twice the amount of money now as before, my lifestyle changed. My attitude of "I CAN'T DO ANYTHING WRONG" followed me into our home. But that was short-lived because my wife got me back down to earth, quickly, fast, and in a hurry. She let me know that I could leave that attitude at work. I was not going to become a dictator over her and our children! Wow, her family had taught her well and the best part of all, she knew how to get her point across without ever raising her voice to me or the kids.

Within a year after my promotion, we bought our second home, a nice 5 bed room house, nice big family room with a large fireplace with plenty of space for everyone. We had an in-ground pool installed shortly after we moved in which added to our family time together. We had Sunday afternoon cookouts after church. We even had several baptisms in our pool. The Lord had truly blessed us beyond words to explain.

Many of our Christian friends would ask how could a young couple with all these children accumulate so much in such a short time.

I couldn't explain it, because it was only a few years ago my credit was so bad I couldn't buy a box of corn flakes on credit. Now I had a large beautiful home with a nice swimming pool, two new cars, four lovely children, and a loving wife.

HOW BLESSED WE WERE, AND WE GAVE ALL THE GLORY TO GOD!

Many nights I would hold Charlotte in my arms as we sat on the deck overlooking the pool during the early summer evenings with the lights of the pool revealing its beauty. The kids were in bed and that was our time together as we fell in love all over again. We would reminisce about where we came from and how we got to where we are now, giving all the glory to our Lord and Savior, Jesus Christ.

I really didn't think our lives could get any better than this. The Lord was using us in our church and in the Gideon Ministries. Charlotte had become a Sunday school teacher, and I was serving as a deacon and a member of the County Jail and Prison Ministries. Even her sister and her family had joined the same church and she was a Sunday school teacher also. We were so happy and blessed.

THE BLESSINGS CONTINUE

One day we read in the local newpapers the city of Maryville was going to extend the main street in this small town in order to connect two major highways. We didn't think too must about it until we learned they would cut right through our farm land which had been in Charlotte's family for years. We sub-cropped that land out over the years, and that was our Christmas-Shopping money. We didn't know how much it was going to affect our holiday income. Besides, my sister-in-law and her family depended on that money much more than we did.

Charlotte replied, "Let's pray about it and give it to the Lord" after she noticed that I was getting all worked up.

A few years later the road construction was complete, and new traffic from the University and St. Louis was growing. The road was the shortcut to the Inter State Hwy. to downtown St. Louis and to SIV. New business was springing up all over the place as a result of the new road.

But it had reduced the amount of crops the farmer could produce and that reduced our income for Christmas money. It had a bigger effect on my sister-in-law and her family than it did on us.

One Saturday morning I attended the Gideons weekly prayer breakfast, and I shared my concerns with my brothers. We made that an item of prayer that morning. A few days later I received a call from a dear Gideon brother by the name Jerry who didn't attend the prayer breakfast but heard of my prayer request. Jerry was a local realtor and had some suggestions for my situation with the farmland. We had lunch one afternoon, and he laid out a plan to sub-divide the land and offer lots for sale and turn it into a subdivision. His plan sounded great!!

Jerry said he could arrange the surveyor, the builders, and the contractors to do all the work. We could pay them a percentage from every lot we sold. In other words, we didn't have to put up one red cent! I couldn't wait to get home to tell my Charlotte.

When I got home, her enthusiasm wasn't as energetic as mine. After all, the land had been in her family all her life, and she was not about to let it slip away just like that. Later that day we had dinner at her mother's home. Her sister and her family were there also. I explained the plan to everyone. There was complete silence!

My nephew, who was about 16 years old, spoke up and said; "THAT WOULD BE NEAT!! It's our land; you can name the streets after us kids." At that point the other kids joined in with their comments.

However, my mother- in-law was a very wise woman. She suggested we pause at that moment and pray about the whole thing. That little lady prayed as if she were talking directly to our Father in heaven, face-to-face.

When she finished praying, all of us were in one accord on the things we should do. First, we must get an attorney to make sure everything is legal from this day forward.

When the construction commenced, we were there for prayer. The entrance of the subdivision was cut, and the first street sign went up with the middle name of our first born: "Renee Dr." The Lord blessed everything during the early construction phase.

Kent put a trailer on the first lot at the entrance to the subdivision and he staffed it noon to five weekdays and 9-5 Saturday and Sunday. We started selling lots faster than the contractor could put the streets in. What a blessing!! Everyone involved were Christian men and women. Charlotte and her sister were there every day with the kids for their Morning Prayer and Devotion. I can tell you, I had never in my entire life seen two likeminded sisters as these two.

The Lord was blessing everything we put out hands to. He was blessing us in church, at home, in my career, and now with our land. It was hard for me to contain the joy and the amount of money that was coming into our household. It came to a point where I started buying everything that came to mind, but my wife kept me balanced. We enjoyed 10 years of prosperity.

DARK DAYS AHEAD

One day when I came home from work, Charlotte was lying on the couch complaining about a severe pain in her lower back. She took some pain pills and went to bed before dinner. That was the first time in our marriage that we didn't sit down and have dinner as a family. Even the kids commented on that. She didn't rest well that night so I took the following day off and took her to see Dr. Kim. He was a Christian man and our family doctor who had been with us during the birth of Christina and death of our twins. Also he was a praying man who believed that Jesus Christ is Lord.

Dr. Kim sent us to Maryville Hospital that morning to have some tests done. Later that afternoon, he called us back to his office to give us the tests results. He explained that Charlotte had advanced colon cancer and it had spread throughout the lower part of her body.

He also explained that the cancer was the result of a ten-year growth, and it was so advanced that treatment would only prolong her life a few months. She looked deep into his eyes and asked, "How long do I have to live, Doctor?" He replied, without hesitation, "Maybe a year."

On our way home, Charlotte asked to stop to get some ice cream and then go sit in the community park in Maryville. It was just the night to eat ice cream and sit outside looking at the stars. We didn't have any concerns for the kids because they were spending the night with their Aunt Carolyn.

We sat there on the park bench eating ice cream for a while not saying anything; I was lost for words. Charlotte opened the conversation in her soft-tone voice by saying we need to tell Carolyn, and we need to talk to the kids. I was up front with her. I told her that I was not ready for this kind of conversation with anyone. Well, that didn't stop her.

The following day she spent the entire day with her sister Carolyn. When I came home that evening, Carolyn was there cooking dinner for the kids.

Charlotte was lying on the couch and all the kids were outside swimming. Carolyn asked me how I was going to handle all the kids' activities and the responsibilities around the house. I was lost for words. All this stuff was happening in our lives so fast, I just couldn't think.

I knew I had to pull myself together because the situation was not going away. Charlotte said that she had a plan. We would talk with the pastor and let the entire church know what was going on. Charlotte didn't want her condition swept under a rug and everyone being afraid to talk about it.

She asked me to take a leave of absence so she could teach me how to handle the affairs of the house. She had the kids involved in everything: Christina in modeling, Amber in dance class, the boys in gymnastics.

I had the hardest time adjusting my thinking to the end results. This is my wife of ten years; this is the mother of my four children! I cried out, "Lord, what is happening to my family???"

Carolyn suggested I hire a grandma-type person to move in with us to help take care of the house and kids. She said the pastor was a good resource if I needed help. They were talking as if they had their plans already in place.

The next question that came to my mind was how were we going to tell the kids, After all, they will begin to see changes in the house and their mother's health.

Charlotte answered that she was going to do it the following day in her own way while no one else was around. She was determined to let them hear the news from her and not someone in church.

I was relieved that she didn't ask me to join her in this conversation because I knew I would break down in front of the children.

A few days later I noticed the kids began to tell me about what was going on with their mother. Christina said, "Dad, mom told us she is going to be with Jesus, and we need to help you around the house."

Each one of them started talking about what each was going to do to help me. I wasn't sure what she told them, but they were excited about helping me.

I learned that she prayed and talked to those kids every single day about the end results and what they needed to do without her being around. She spent more time talking with Christina, because she was the oldest (10), and the other three usually followed her lead.

It only took a few days to find a grandma-type lady to move in with us. The kids were excited. Her name was Vivian, a Christian lady with six grandkids of her own. Her grandchildren came over to the house often, and they became to be like family. They even started attending our church.

Each day we had a house full of people. No one would have believed based on her attitude, that this mother only had a few months to live. There were songs of joy, prayer, fellowship, and plenty of food every day.

All our Christian friends who came over left with a smile and gave me some encouraging words: **Romans 8:28: "And we know that ALL THINGS WORK TOGETHER FOR GOOD TO THEM THAT LOVE GOD, TO THEM WHO ARE CALLED ACCORDING TO HIS PURPOSE."**

I heard that scripture so much, I got sick of hearing it because I could not understand what good could come out of my losing my best friend and the mother of my four children. It just didn't make any sense to me at all. Within nine months, the Lord called Charlotte home at the age of 32.

During the memorial service, the kids and I stood up front as our guests passed by to view the body and pay their last respects. Some of our non-Christian friends broke down as they passed, and some commented later; "HOW COULD THOSE CHILDREN HOLD THEMSELVES TOGETHER LIKE THAT AFTER LOSING THEIR MOTHER TO CANCER?"

Rev. Crouch gave a powerful message of salvation, and when the invitation came, hands went up from across the auditorium to accept Jesus as their Lord and Savior.

Later that day, I had a replay in my mind of all those people in attendance during the memorial service and the number of hands that were raised to accept Christ. It occurred to me, "Maybe that was the reality of Romans 8:28: **'And we know that all things work together for good to them that love God, to them who are the called according to his purpose.'**

Many of our non-Christian friends had never attended church to hear a message of salvation. And maybe the Lord used Charlotte's death to accomplish His will.

Lord, we don't understand everything that takes place in our lives, but one thing for sure: Your word is true!

Isaiah 55:8-9 (KJV): "For my thoughts *are* not your thoughts, neither *are* your ways my ways, saith the Lord.

For as the heavens are higher than the earth, so are my ways higher than your ways, and my thoughts than your thoughts.

For as the rain cometh down, and the snow from heaven, and returneth not thither, but watereth the earth, and maketh it bring forth and bud, that it may give seed to the sower, and bread to the eater:

So shall my word be that goeth forth out of my mouth: it shall not return unto me void, but it shall accomplish that which I please, and it shall prosper *in the thing* whereto I sent it."

A few weeks after Charlotte's death, I was collecting her personal items when I ran across her well-used Bible. When I picked it up, a three-page letter fell out of it. Two of the pages were written to each of the children and the day she prayed and led each one of them to Christ. She noted that this was her assurance that she would see them again. The third page was written to me. She opened her letter with a greeting from the word of God: **ROMANS 8:28!**

WHILE READING THAT, I FELL TO MY KNEES BESIDE THE BED AND BEGAN TO CRY AND BEAT ON THE BED WITH MY FIST.

I CRIED: LORD, HOW CAN YOU SAY THAT SOMETHING GOOD WILL COME FROM LOSING MY BEST FRIEND AND THE MOTHER OF MY

FOUR CHILDREN?? AT THAT MOMENT, I FELT THE PEACE OF GOD ALL OVER ME. PRAISE YOUR HOLY NAME!!

This was our first family photo after their mother passed away. Leroy, Amber (age 6) Michael (age 8), Christina Renee (age 11) Robert (age 10).

A HOME WITHOUT A MOM

During the weeks following Charlotte's death, our lives began to take on new meaning. The kids were involved in their after school and weekend activities and my career was moving right along. Our live-in housekeeper was working day and night to keep up with the kids' activities and house work. I could tell that it was stressing her out at times.

One night I worked late, and she met me in the kitchen when I walked into the house. She asked to speak with me about the kids. She went on to explain how their behavior was getting out of control. The boys were non-compliant, and Amber was following in their footsteps at her early age. She went on to explain how Christiana had started talking back and telling her, "This is not the way my mother did things around the house."

I could see her frustration at that point, but I was not prepared for what followed. She gave me a two-week notice. She didn't give me an opportunity to reply. She turned and walked out of the kitchen.

After she left me standing there, I had to sit down to recap all the things she told me; especially the part concerning the kids' behavior.

I wasn't sure what I was going to do at that point because I thought Vivian would be with us until the kids got older. Her notice came at a time when it would be a big setback for me about managing my household because I didn't have a clue where to start.

The following night I talked with my pastor after the evening service. He listened and we prayed about the situation, but he didn't have any advice. Later I talked with a few of my Christian friends, and a few of them said they would help until I could find someone to take Vivian's place. That was not the answer I was looking for.

One night I came home late, and I heard crying from the girls' bedroom. I knocked and walked in slowly. Christina was sitting up in her bed with her legs crossed, crying.

I sat down beside her, and she gave me a big hug but she started crying profusely. I didn't say anything. I just let her get it all out. Once she settled down, I asked what was wrong.

She replied; "Dad I miss Mom. I wish you were home more." At that, Amber jumped off her bed and onto my lap. She began crying and spoke in agreement with her sister. "Yes, Dad, we want you home to eat dinner with us like we used to do when Mom was here."

We talked for a while; then we went into the kitchen and made a few PB and J sandwiches and had a glass of milk. The boys heard us in the kitchen and they joined in.

As we sat around the table eating PB and J and drinking milk, the boys voiced their opinions concerning the amount of time I spent with them. It was more Bobby than Michael because his mouth was full. They were talking as if they had talked about this among themselves before.

I paid close attention to their concerns, but in my mind, all of this was coming at the wrong time, especially after talking with Vivian a few nights ago. I told them I would think about their requests and we would work something out as a family. That made all of them very happy. We had prayer and went to bed.

I couldn't sleep at all that night. My kids wanted me home more often to fill the void in their lives; my housekeeper had given me a two-week notice.

I had just gotten a promotion as Unit Manager to a new Kroger Super Sav-On Supercenter in South St. Louis. All of these things were going through my mind at a hundred miles an hour, and I didn't have a solution how to make it work. I didn't fall asleep that night until after 3 a.m.

As I was getting ready for work the following morning, a strange feeling came over me. It was if I were doing something wrong by going to work, and that feeling stayed with me throughout the day. I couldn't explain that feeling because I loved my job. Besides, I was on a fast track to become Regional Manager of 125 stores in one of the company's divisions. Each day that feeling of guilt continued to get more intense.

The following Sunday the kids and I went forward during the morning church service for prayer. That was a blessed time as the church leaders laid hands on us and prayed. Christina and Amber were crying with tears of joy afterwards. It blessed my heart to see my little girls so in tune with prayer and the word of God. After church, we went to the mall for lunch with some close friends.

As I was getting ready for work that Monday morning, my feeling of disobedience was intensifying. During the afternoon, I was conducting a management meeting. Just then the thought continued to haunt me: I was not doing what the Lord wanted me to do. Finally, the conviction was so great I just couldn't handle it any more. After I spent time in my office praying about the conviction that I was under, the Lord gave me the answer. I didn't understand it, but I knew I had to obey.

Later that day I called my Regional Manager and told him that I was giving my notice. It blew his mind!

He said, "I know you lost your wife a short time ago, but are you losing your mind?" He asked; "Did you strike it rich with a payoff on an insurance policy? Do you need some time off to think this over? I can't believe we are having this conversation. I'll see you in the morning, and we can get this resolved."

On my way home that evening, I FELT GREAT! I couldn't explain it. I had just quit my job, and I don't have a source of income to support my family. Yet, I feel great. I didn't understand it, but I was free of any convictions!

When I got home, I told the kids what I had done, and they were jumping with joy. Amber said, "You mean you don't have to go to work anymore, Dad."

Christina gave me a big hug and a smile; "I'm so happy, I LOVE YOU, DAD!"

The following morning I met with my Regional Manager and I gave him my resignation in writing: effective immediately. He knew by the tone of my voice that my decision was final. He accepted my resignation without any further discussion.

That following Saturday morning, I attended my regular Saturday Morning Prayer Breakfast, and I told my brothers in Christ of my decision. I explained that I didn't have a clue of how I was going to support my family long-term, but Charlotte's life insurance would sustain us for about a year.

One of the brothers said, "Leroy, let's pray about God's directions for your life and that of your children."

That morning we had a very good time of prayer and fellowship.

Within two months after I left The Kroger Company, they sold their entire St. Louis Division of over 130 stores, a large office complex, and a distribution center. Hundreds of Managers and thousands of hourly associates lost their jobs.

This was the first week that I was home with the kids. It was also the first week we had been without Vivian. I was so glad this was a time of summer vacation because I was not familiar with their school schedule. I cooked breakfast that morning, and we enjoyed that time of interaction with each other.

Christina made a comment: "This is the way we were when Mom was here." All the others agreed. I gave them a schedule of our day of grocery shopping, but they had to clean the house first. They loved that plan because this is something they did when their mother was around.

I asked them to explain some of the things they did during the day with mom. I wanted them to talk about all the fun things they did with their Mother because I noticed how much of a positive attitude they had when this happened. So from that point on, I asked them to put together a daily activity calendar so all of us were on the same page. We left room for flexibility to change it if we all agreed. We spent that morning cleaning and making plans for the summer.

That afternoon we went grocery shopping. Christina was pushing the shopping buggy, and I was doing the grocery shopping (without a list).

I was putting items in the cart when Christina said,

"Dad, Mom didn't shop like that." I turned around and all four of them were staring at me with that blank look in their eyes.

"OK, show me how Mom shopped?" Christina went on to explain that mom had a list and she shopped by meals.

I wanted them to feel good about our time together so I asked them to teach me everything their mother had taught them so I could learn also.

Their faces lit up with joy! I told Christina from now on, she would make the grocery list and she would put the items in the cart. I would push the shopping cart. She loved that idea!! From that point on, my 12-year-old daughter became the mother of the house and the other kids followed her lead.

Amber was the only one who would argue that she was too "BOSSY!"

That's when I stepped in to keep a balance. (Things with those two are the same now as it was back in that day.)

We had our daily duties mapped out, and everything was moving along very well without a housekeeper. We had an agreement: no swimming, no company or outside activities until the house was clean and we had breakfast. All of them did their part.

Amber loved to vacuum the pool each morning, and she was not about to give that up no matter what the others had to say. She did a good job, so I had no complaints.

I learned quickly how most parents would drop their kids off to go swimming, and I became the neighborhood babysitter. Some of them would stay seven or eight hours a day. That meant I had to feed them and also give them snacks. This became too much like work. This was something that Vivian had started, and I'm sure it contributed to her stress. Later that evening as we were having dinner, I asked the kids, "Did Mom let all your friends come over every day and swim?"

Christina said that mom would only let them come over if their mother or older brothers or sisters were with them. That way it wasn't so many kids in the pool, but Vivian didn't care.

I told them: starting tomorrow they needed to get the word out to their friends the way their mother did it. The following day, we had the entire pool to ourselves-all day!

The summer was moving along without any complications in our family life. The kids and I became even closer. I could see how our relationship had changed. I could see how the Lord used me to step into their lives when they needed a mom and dad the most. I believe the Lord used those nine months, leading up to their mother's death, to work them into a daily lifestyle without her but help them to maintain the same quality of lifestyle that she laid out for them.

The Lord used our time together to work me into their daily routine ...THANK YOU, LORD JESUS, FOR YOUR CONTINUED SUPPORT!!

During that summer, there were a few other things they taught me. One night as I was reviewing the payroll on the construction job, Amber came into the room and asked me something. I didn't really listen to what she said, but I said, OK! About an hour later I was walking down the hallway, I saw Amber with one of these these big sassier cuts of Christina's hair. I HIT THE ROOF!! I asked, WHAT IN THE WORLD ARE YOU DOING?? Amber replied in a tearful voice, "I asked you if Christina and I could cut our hair, and you said yes." I was lost for words after she said that.

There I was standing there looking at all that beautiful black hair all over the floor. If their mother were still alive and I had done that, she would have hung me out the window by my toe nails. Their hair was her pride and joy.

Another one of my lessons learned as a single parent: you must clean the filter in the dryer after every load. Too bad I didn't learn this lesson until after I bought a new one, because it was taking hours to dry a small load.

We did every conceivable thing that I thought Charlotte would do with them during the summer. They attended VBS each week going to every church in the community. On weekends we had cookouts, swim parties, and we enjoyed our season tickets to Six Flags over Mid-America. We went to the zoo and all the tourist attractions in the St. Louis area. They never got bored. I made sure their lives were filled with all the activities they enjoyed with their mother, Aunt Carolyn, and their cousin Dawn.

Well, summer was coming to an end, and it was approaching back-to-school time. I was beat from all the summer activities, and I thought this was a time that I could get some rest during the day while they were in school. It had slipped my mind concerning all their fall and winter activities. I was hoping they would forget or just lose interest. Great thought, but it didn't happen!

They attended private Christian school about 15 miles from our home. During their first week of school, they came home with all these papers for me to sign for after-school activities. They were so excited when they got home as they explained how their mother took them here and there and helped their teachers to transport other kids on field trips. It was at that point that I realized that I could not keep up with all the things their mother did. During dinner that evening, I had to admit to all of them that I just couldn't do it. I couldn't keep up with their expectations with everything their mother did. I went on to explain that we had to move forward, and we had to make changes in our daily lifestyle. They had this intense look on their faces as I spoke, and there was complete silence among them. I told them that I could do some of those things but not all. I told them that I couldn't play the role of mom and dad any more, but I promised them that I would be the best dad that any kid could ask for. After I made that statement, Amber got up and walked around the table and gave me a big hug. The other three got up and I found myself on the floor with four kids all over me telling me how much they loved me.

The girls decided to continue with dance and Pee-Wee football for the boys. That worked just fine for me because there were several families in our church who had kids participating in the same activities, and they offered to take them to and from their practices.

NEW DIRECTIONS

By this time I had started thinking about what I was going to do for an income because I was not at that high level salary as before. I attended my regular Saturday Morning Prayer Breakfast, and I shared my concerns with my brothers in Christ. We made my situation a matter of prayer, and within ten days, the Lord had answered our prayers.

Our subdivision wasn't growing as fast as it did in the beginning. After only a few years, we had only sold six homes and one street "RENEE DR." The area looked great, but Kent had stopped staffing it on weekends, and the builder had run into financial difficulties. Also, he didn't have the backing to build several homes to be a display as he had done in the beginning. Things had really slowed down; however, the subdivision was never a source of income that we depended on during the years.

One day I got a call from a co-worker from The Kroger Company. She told me that she had opened an agency for Century 21 and she wanted to know if I would list my property with her. She knew that I was working with Kent and assured me that there would not be any conflicts. She went on to explain how she had two builders who wanted to put several spec homes on my property. I didn't see any reason why this couldn't work, so I agreed.

Within a short period, our lot sales tripled over the year before. The Lord had provided us with an income that surpassed what I was making as a Manager for The Kroger Company. My sister-in-law's income more than doubled after our lot sales took off. She then quit her job as a retail manager for K-Mart.

The Lord had provided as only He could!! He kept his promise to me ... Isaiah 1:19: "If ye be willing and obedient, ye shall eat the good from the land."

I secured a live-in housekeeper to take care of the house, but I took the kids to school and picked them up. Our time together didn't change, and they were happy.

I wanted something to do with my extra time, so I decided to get involved with my sub-division and become a builder in order to cut out the middle man. I attended classes at SIV to help sharpen my business, organizational and managerial skills in construction. The instructor said that she was keen on why people wanted to change careers during middle age. She and I took a liking to each other, and she pointed me into the direction of becoming a government contractor. She was right on with all the information she provided. Within a few months, I was bidding on government construction projects.

There was a man I knew by the name of Dan who had done work on our church. He was a construction manager, but he had lost his job due to his wife's illness. I thought the Lord brought us together so I hired him as my construction manager for government contracts. (I didn't consult with my Saturday Morning Prayer Partners as I had done so many times in the past.)

Our first few jobs we bid were under $20,000. Everything went well and the job came in below bid; therefore, we made a nice profit.

I was happy with jobs in this price range because it didn't strain our cash flow. The only problem with government work is the waiting time to get paid for work completed. You are told during pre-construction meetings, you will receive your money 15 days after each phase of the work is completed. That works out fine if you have enough money in the bank to cover your weekly payroll.

One night Dan invited me over to his house for dinner. I really enjoyed his wife's cooking. After dinner we went into his study, and he had a bunch of plans and blue prints lying across his desk. He started explaining about some of the work we could bid on and make a big profit. I was all ears as he continued. After all, this was his area of expertise.

The job was close to $900,000. He showed me how we could bring this job in and clear over $250.000 in less than a year on this one job. Wow, this sounded great. This was more money than I was making on my own.

The only catch: we were a sub-contractor for a larger construction company. This would be the first time we had been a sub-contractor, and we had to wait an extra seven days to get paid for work completed. That meant we needed enough money in the bank each week to cover our payroll.

When I left Dan's house that evening, I wasn't sure why I was feeling under conviction. Something was wrong, but I didn't know what.

By the time we started that $900,000 project, we had three or four smaller government jobs going on, and I had also started building homes in my sub-division. Everything was moving right along, but each day the conviction remained.

During my time with my Christian Brothers on Saturday Morning, our conversation had become more of what I was doing rather than asking for prayer. It was all about me and my efforts. There was no focus on my Lord and Savior Jesus Christ. It was all about me, me, me, and me!!! I had forgotten about where I had been and how I had gotten to where I was at this point.

One night after the evening service, the pastor asked me if I would consider going on a mission trip to India for a few weeks. He asked me to pray about it and let him know in a few days.

On my way home, I thought maybe that would do me good if I went on a mission trip to India. I didn't want the kids to hear about the pastor's request from one of their friends, so we stopped by McDonald's, for a snack.

When I told them what the pastor asked us to do, they were excited. Amber asked, "When are we leaving, Dad?" The other three joined in with their questions and comments. When I told them that they couldn't go, there were no more comments. They settled down and finished eating their food. I knew that conversation was not over, but I left it there.

Later that night after they went to bed, I called Carolyn (Charlotte's sister) to tell her about the mission trip and to get her input. By this time, she had purchased a nice home from the money we got from the sales of the lots in the sub-division. Now she didn't think that I could do anything wrong. We talked about the mission trip, and she came up with a plan for the kids. She would visit them every day to make sure everything in the house was going on without any complication.

Our housekeeper had been with us for over a year and the kids loved and respected her. During the month leading up to my departure, I visited with Dan many times, and we put together a thirty-day plan to cover the payroll for the big job. I had arranged a $50,000 line of credit, but I had to put up my sub-division as security. After covering all the details with Dan, Carolyn, and my housekeeper, I was off to India with Pastor Tom and Pastor Mark.

THE MISSION TRIP

This was a big deal for me because I had never traveled outside the country. We had plans to visit two other countries, Sri Lanka and Pakistan during our 30-day trip. This was a big adjustment for me: the heat, the bugs, the food, and the living conditions were something I had never experienced. But I fell right in with the locals. At times, we dressed just like them so we didn't look like outsiders. During our trip, we visited churches, nursing homes, hospitals, and orphanages, in the cities and village areas. It was not a trip where we stayed in a five-star hotel. We lived in their homes, and we slept on bamboo mats rolled out on the floor just as they did. I witnessed sickness and living conditions far beyond what words can explain.

I can relate first hand to the words of Jesus:

Matthew 9:36-38: "But when he saw the multitudes, he was moved with compassion on them, because they fainted, and were scattered abroad, as sheep having no shepherd.

Then saith he unto his disciples, The harvest truly is plenteous, but the labourers are few.

Pray ye therefore the Lord of the harvest, that he will send forth labourers into his harvest."

I thank you, Lord Jesus, for opening my eyes during this mission trip.

After 10 days in India, we went down to Colombo, Sri Lanka, to work and encourage the brothers in that country. Sri Lanka is a strong Buddhist country, and they don't take kindly to outsiders coming and disturbing their culture and lifestyle.

We were very careful as we worked with the brothers in Colombo. They had informed us earlier of the violence as a result of the civil war between the Senegalese Government and the Tamil rebels. The brothers working in the country had arranged meetings in many house churches in the city and village areas. There were so many hungry souls attending the meetings, they would fill the entire house even if they couldn't see the speaker. They just wanted to hear the word of God and have a time of prayer.

During our trip, I didn't have a regular speaking part, but I would share parts of my testimony as the Lord would lead, and I would pray for believers and new converts. I was blessed when I saw the response as a result of Pastor Tom's and Pastor Mark's messages. Our days were long, mostly due to heavy traffic as we were trying to get around the city. We had to travel very early in the morning and late during the evening hours in order to cover any distance.

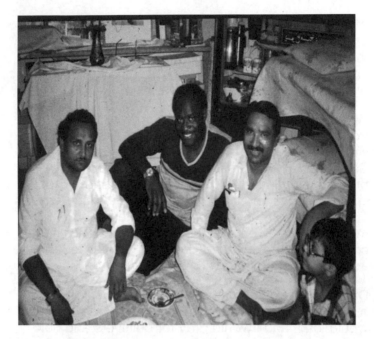

We concluded our trip by visiting the Brothers in Peshawar, Pakistan. We had about the amount of freedom to share the Gospel in that country as we had in Sri Lanka. However, most of the house church congregations were professional men, and church services were held in their homes because of their size.

We didn't see the illness and poverty in Pakistan as we had seen in India and Sri Lanka. Our focus in that country was on meetings with pastors and church leaders. Pastor Mark was a specialist in training church leaders with a focus on church growth.

After a week, we left Pakistan heading home. It was a long journey, and we didn't say too much to each other about our trip. We were buried deep in thoughts concerning the needs. All I could think about was the villagers in Sri Lanka. I was broken hearted after seeing the needs those people had for feeding centers just to get food, a simple medical station to get antibiotics, the need for homes made with bricks for the needy.

My heart was on fire to help those people, but I didn't know how.

When we returned to the States, we went our separate ways; but after a few weeks, we got together to recap our trip. By this time, we had collected our thoughts and put some priorities in place concerning a future mission trip. That was all good for them, but I didn't have any plans to return on another mission trip going anywhere, but I would support others if they wanted to go.

Pastor Mark explained how the Lord was leading him to return to Pakistan to work with the area pastors there. Pastor Tom had kept in touch with several churches in India and was going back to work with them to help plant new churches. Also, he wanted to sponsor several new pastors to come to the States so they could receive more training. It seemed as if they had met with the Lord, and all their plans were in place.

They asked if the Lord were dealing with me concerning mission work. I told them that I had a burden for work in Sri Lanka, but I had no intention of returning. I explained there was a brother from Colombo who wrote me requesting that I return to work with him. He said that he believed the Lord brought us together for a reason, but he didn't go into details to explain. I told him that I would help to raise finances to support his work.

After our meeting, we had prayer and went our separate ways.

LORD, WHAT'S NEXT?

A few months had passed since we returned from our mission trip, but I still had this burden for the work in Sri Lanka. One evening I booked a call to Sri Lanka to speak with the brothers I had met at one of the mission houses.

After that conversation, my burden was even greater. I prayed that evening, asking the Lord to lighten the load that I was carrying with my family, my business, and now with overseas mission work. It was more than I could handle, and it was wearing me down. I was getting frustrated and confused. It got to a point that I resigned from the mission board at church because I didn't want to talk about mission work anymore.

Our construction project was going good, and the lots in the sub-division were selling at a steady pace. Dan said he wanted us to bid another piece of the job with the same contractor. He went on to explain how this work would yield a good profit and make the name of our company, "NEW TECH ENTERPRISE" a household name in the construction business.

I was relying on his experience to complete the work timely, and on my experience to handle the finances. I agreed with his decision without looking at the details of the contract and our financial obligations.

I attended my Saturday Morning Prayer Meeting, and I shared with my brothers about all the things that were going on in my life and how they were wearing me down. It wasn't the family or the business, but the burden of mission work overseas, which was causing me to lose focus on everything else. I asked for prayer that morning. They could see that I was heavily laden.

By this time I had learned that Pastor Mark and Pastor Tom had followed through on what the Lord had put on their hearts. They returned to the mission field to India and Pakistan to do the work they were called to do.

During the winter months, our construction work closed down and it wasn't scheduled to reopen until the Spring.

Dan and I agreed that we needed another site supervisor, and he said he had one in mind. His name was Willie. I didn't know it but learned later that Willie had a background. He had done time for armed robbery and drug possession.

At the beginning of our construction season in the Spring, one of my Saturday Morning Prayer Partners suggested that I should get with all my business associates and have a time of prayer before the season began. I thought that was a great idea, so when I got home that morning, I started putting together a list of Christian associates who worked for me. What an eye-opener! I didn't have any!

During my pursuit for success, I had pushed all of my Christian associates out of my business, and now I was surrounded by non-Christians. I had pushed Kent out of the sub-division by bringing in Century 21. I did the same thing with my Christian builders also. Over the course of time, I had done the same thing with the workers in my construction company. These were the people the Lord had surrounded me with from the beginning. Now all of them were gone.

My life had gotten out of control. I did what pleased me. I was trafficking in affairs with single mothers, but I managed to keep them under the table and away from my children. Most of them were looking for a good catch and most of them came on strong. To them it seemed that I had it all, a nice home and was financially sound. I slipped back into the world system almost without my knowledge.

I realized that I didn't have anyone working for my company to pray with as we had done in the beginning. I had even isolated myself from my Lord and Savior by resigning from the mission board at my church and turned away from mission work.

My eyes were opened, and I realized that it had been all about me and what I wanted. I had lost all sensitivity concerning the direction the Lord was leading me. I had ignored the things that He was putting on my heart. Pastor Tom and Pastor Mark were obedient enough to follow the Lord's leading, but I wasn't.

We opened our construction season with a lot of activities going on simultaneously, and the financial strain on my bank account was more that I had planned for. We had a large start-up cost of bringing in heavy equipment and the payroll for heavy equipment operators and other factors we hadn't planned. I had to use my sub-division as security to get the finances to cover my expenses until I had a cash flow coming in. But that didn't happen because the General Contractor we worked for filed for bankruptcy within one month after construction season opened. He left us holding a $1.5m contract, and he owed us over $150,000. We were not set up to handle that kind of out-of-pocket loss as a small contractor.

From that point, everything I touched turn into mud, financially speaking. Within 6 months, I had lost my business, and the bank cashed in on my sub-division to cover my outstanding line of credit. The only thing I had left was my home.

This was a bad time for me. I couldn't think, and I did not have a prayer life! I was devastated mentally!!

During my weekly Saturday Morning Prayer Breakfasts, I shared some of details of my issues with my brothers. One suggested I put together a business plan for a repayment plan and meet with my creditors and seek a second chance. Another suggested I get away from it all and pray for guidance. Then others spoke in agreement with prayer, but one added, a time of fasting also.

I told my children and my sister-in-law that I had to get away for a few days on business. My sister-in-law was not aware of the loss that I had caused with the sub-division. She had trusted me with her livelihood and now, I had let her down. I really didn't know where to turn. I didn't believe that even God could undo the mess that I had gotten myself into.

After I finalized my plans with the housekeeper, I got into my car early the next morning before the kids got up and started driving without a destination in mind. I drove for hours, before I realized, I was in the Lake of the Ozarks someplace in southwestern MO. I checked into a motel and decided that this was going to be the place where I spent time seeking guidance from the Lord.

After I checked into the motel, I tried to pray but the words wouldn't come because I could not stop thinking about my losses. I could not stop thinking about the people I had turned my back on during my blind state of making money. I was angry with myself, and there were times when I was angry with God. I was hurting!!!!!!! I just didn't know how to pray or what to say! I was in a state of loneliness and confusion.

I sat down at the desk next to my bed, and I thought it would be a good time to work on that repayment plan to present to my creditors to keep from losing my empire. I thought that I could work myself out of this mess without praying. But the more I worked on the business plan, the more confusing it got. I couldn't even make sense of my own plan so how was I going to explain it to my bankers. After working on it for a few hours, I got so frustrated, I ripped it up in small pieces crying, cursing, and kicking the bed stand.

After a while, I calmed down. My eyes were blood red when I looked into the bathroom mirror. I was beat from the long drive! I was feeling as if someone had beaten my body all over wearing boxing gloves, so I went to bed, but I only slept a few hours. I was tossing and turning in bed and the thoughts that were going through my mind were more than I could handle. I couldn't lie there! I had to get up. I opened the desk drawer looking for another note pad because I had ripped up the other one; however, there was a brand new brown covered Bible which said: Placed by The Gideons. I picked up that Bible and I sat back on my bed.

There was a page folded in the book of Proverbs and that is where I started reading (Proverbs 15). The first nine verses of this proverb cut right through me as I read!!

A gentle answer turns away wrath,
But a [a]harsh word stirs up anger.
2 The tongue of the wise makes knowledge [b]acceptable,
But the mouth of fools spouts folly.
3 The eyes of the LORD are in every place,
watching the evil and the good.
4 A [c]soothing tongue is a tree of life,
but perversion in it [d]crushes the spirit.
5 A fool [e]rejects his father's discipline,
But he who regards reproof is sensible.
6 Great wealth is in the house of the righteous,
But trouble is in the income of the wicked.
7 The lips of the wise spread knowledge,
But the hearts of fools are not so.
8 The sacrifice of the wicked is an abomination to the LORD,
But the prayer of the upright is His delight.
9 The way of the wicked is an abomination to the LORD,
But He loves one who pursues righteousness.

I had focused more on my plans, my needs, and I had forgotten about my Maker. It was then when I realized that I was a sinner! Conviction was so heavy that night. I fell to my knees and began to cry out to the

Lord, asking for forgiveness by His grace and mercy. I prayed for hours in that hotel room pouring my heart out to the Lord. This had been the second time in my life that the Lord used a Gideon scripture from a Gideon-placed Bible to speak to my heart and change my life.

I'm not sure how long I spent praying that night, but when I got up, I felt like a new person. It was like the first time when I met Jesus in that park in Battle Creek, Michigan. I continued to read the word of God all during the night. The more I read, the better I felt. I fell asleep and slept like a baby that night without a care in the world.

The next morning during my time of devotion, I prayed and dedicated everything that I had to Him. I was in a state of total surrender, and it felt great knowing that He was taking over my life, my family, and my personal and business affairs. I felt good knowing that He would get the mess that I had made of life worked out. I didn't care about anything except following Him. LORD, I SURRENDER ALL!!

That following day I knew that I had a breakthrough in my situation, and the peace of God was all over me. On my drive home, I continued to pray and seek His will for my life.

I stopped by the sub-division and had a time of prayer. During that prayer time, I was not telling the Lord what I wanted. It was all about His will being done in my life and in my business.

Over the next few months, I watched as all the material things were taken away from me. I cannot explain it, but there was the peace of God all over me during that process. The wisdom of the Lord helped me to settle matters with my banks without a court battle over who gets what. This was a smooth transition with a feeling of perfect peace in the whole process. I cannot explain why, but I knew the Lord was in control.

My relationship with my sister-in-law had fallen apart, but she remained close to the kids.

A few days after I closed all my business affairs, I received a letter from the dear brother I worked with in Sri Lanka during my mission trip. He expressed his need for my help. This time I listened. The Lord spoke to my heart as I began to entertain the thought of what I could do to help his cause. Later that day, I met with my pastor and told him what the Lord was putting on my heart concerning mission work in Sri Lanka. He said he could not tell me what to do; however, he would pray with me for God's wisdom and direction for my life. After he left, I spent the rest of the day in prayer. The house was empty so I had that time alone with God!

A CALL FOR COMMITMENT

Returning to Sir Lanka on another mission trip was becoming more and more real to me, but I was not sure for how long and at what cost. Then there was the welfare of the kids. I did not know what I was going to do with them because I had let the housekeeper go since I could not afford to pay her salary. I had no income. All these questions were going through my mind at a 100 mph, and I was not coming up with any answers.

I thought it would be best if I called this brother, tell him of my loss, and explain to him why it would be impossible for me to return to Sri Lanka. After we talked, we concluded with prayer. He prayed as if he were talking directly to the Lord. Each word he spoke cut deeply into my spirit, and I came under conviction.

That following Saturday Morning at prayer breakfast, I shared my burden with my brothers in the Lord. There was a group of men with strong commitments to the Lord. They were men of the Book and men of Prayer. They had known me from the first night my wife and I joined this association of Christian Business and Professional men. They had witnessed the ups and downs in my life, including the death of my wife. We had developed a relationship built on the word of God and trust. I valued their prayers and comments. I shared with them the burden the Lord had put on my heart concerning mission work in Sri Lanka, but I went on to explain that I had a lot of questions.

Ernie was always the first one to reply when there was a need. "Let's pray about it!" was his solution. Ernie was a real prayer warrior, and I had been a witness to so many of his answered prayers.

After prayer, we had breakfast. That was the time we shared our thoughts as the Lord led concerning prayer requests. One of the brothers suggested that I solicit financial support from local churches. After all, I was not a stranger to any of them.

Another brother explained that his church had a new pastor who was on fire for missions. He thought his church in Maryville would be supportive.

Another brother suggested I take my kids on the trip. He explained how most missionaries travel with their families on the mission field. Wow, all the things they spoke were coming at me with such clarity. They answered many questions that had bothered me for weeks.

Several days later, I went over to have dinner with Ernie and his wife. I really looked up to Ernie because he was my spiritual father, and his wife was my mother in the Lord. Both of them had been the encouragement that Charlotte and I needed during our early walk with the Lord and with the Gideon Ministry. After dinner, we had a time of prayer. I left his house that evening with a renewed attitude and more confidence about serving the Lord on the mission field.

I did not waste any time contacting churches for support. Some pledged monthly, and others were willing to give a one-time donation. I had lunch with the pastor of the Maryville Church, a real man of God, who gave me a generous donation from his church missions' committee. (A few years later, someone walked into the morning service and shot him to death.)

The next hurdle I had to overcome was breaking the news to my children (ages 7-13). I was not sure how they were going to handle it. After all, I was about to ask them to move half way around the world and give up the only lifestyle they were accustomed to.

After church that Sunday, I got us a bucket of fried chicken, and we had dinner at home. I told them I wanted to show them a slide show of when I was on my mission trip. Michael complained that I had shown it to them before, but the girls were all for it. Earlier that morning, I had asked my Sunday school class to pray for me concerning mission work, but I did not share the details of my request.

We were enjoying our time together that afternoon, laughing, telling jokes, and eating chicken, I made a joke about living in another country. All of them thought that was funny. The girls opened up the conversation about living in India and Sri Lanka. They thought it would be neat! I picked up the conversation from that point and shared my burden of moving to Sri Lanka, working with some of village people.

Amber asked, "What about us Dad? Will you take us with you?"

"If you decide to go, I want you to know that your life will not be the same as it is here. You would not have any of your favorite eating places, and it's hot, and you wouldn't have air conditioning!"

Christiana responded by saying, "All that stuff doesn't matter as long as we are together."

Before anyone could say another word, Bobby replied; "I THINK WE SHOULD PRAY ABOUT THAT!" We all agreed to pray and leave the rest up to the Lord. We never got around to watching the slides.

We spent the rest of the day relaxing around the house; the girls were glued to my hip. They made comments about how they could help. They wanted to use their puppets in a way to win the village kids to Christ. They had their own puppet stage ready to go. Now that was something that I had never thought of. After all, they were members of the puppet team at church. Just think: A family missionary team from the States using puppets as an outreach tool for crusades for Christ.

The more I thought about it, the more it seemed possible. When the boys heard the girls and me talking about puppets, they jumped in and claimed their positions working with the puppets. All of this was my confirmation to proceed.

Later that evening we went over to Carolyn's house and broke the news to her. She told me that I was out of my mind by taking the kids away from their homeland. She suggested that I go but leave the kids with her. When she made that statement, they spoke up, "We want to go with Dad, Aunt Carolyn." Based on their response, she knew they would not be satisfied staying with her. She offered her support for *them*; my name was still mud in her book.

The following day I had lunch with my dear friend and authority John. I covered the details of my mission plans with him, but I needed his advice on how to handle my home. I had thought of renting it out, but he strongly advised me not to. I really did not want to sell it because it was our home, and we would need a place to live when we returned. There I was, still wanting to hold on the material things instead of trusting the Lord. When we concluded our meeting, he had my power of attorney to close the deal on my house in case it did not sell until after we left the country. The following day it was listed with a Christian realtor.

I booked a call to Sri Lanka and laid out my travel plans with my brother in Christ. I told him I needed him to find us a place to live in Colombo and locate an international school for the kids. He was so excited to learn that I was coming and bringing my entire family. It was a time of rejoicing on both ends. I felt good about the whole situation. I knew the Lord was in this plan because from that point on, every decision and move were timely.

Our home had been on the market for six weeks and still no offers. It was nearing the time for us to leave, so we decided to have an estate sale to clean out everything we had in the house. The realtor thought this would be a great opportunity to promote an open house also. She ran ads in the local paper and mailed flyers to promote the open house. That was a very big weekend. I never had so many people walking through my house at one time. I was sure the realtor would get some serious offers on the property, but nothing happened. We were packed and ready to depart on Tuesday. Our prayer life was very strong during those two days leading up to our trip. On the day of our departure, we got up early and I asked Amber to lead us in prayer. I can tell you that little six-year-old girl touched my heart with her soft-spoken words for our trip and the sale of our home.

The realtor pulled into the driveway as we were loading our 12 duffel bags into my brother-in-Christ's pickup truck. She jumped out of the car with excitement in her voice and on her face. She explained that she had worked with a couple into the late hours of the night to reach a deal on my home. They were already pre-approved for more than our asking price, and they wanted to close the deal today.

The kids and I starting praising the Lord because it was just a short time ago my little six-year-old girl had prayed for a closing on our home. I told the realtor that we had a flight to catch, but my attorney had my power of attorney to close the deal.

What a mighty God we serve! Never late! Always on time!!

After receiving that news from the realtor, I felt good about the entire missionary situation. A new confirmation that the Lord was in this plan. Everything fell into place!

We departed from JFK airport on Tuesday morning at 10:20 a.m. and arrived in Sri Lanka two days later. My brother in Christ, Ronsillaga, had everything in place and ready for our arrival. He did not waste any time with small talk. He laid out the schedule for the next few weeks. He wanted to start working as soon as we got settled in.

The kids were in a state of unbelief of the living conditions, but they did not complain *much*. That night after we had dinner, the kids went to bed early. After all, there was absolutely nothing to do except watch the stars. I could hear them talking among themselves in the other room. We had a white rented house with only two bedrooms, a small kitchen, and a small bathroom without running water. All the electricity in the area would be turned off at certain times to conserve energy.

Just when I was about half asleep, I heard a loud scream coming from the kids' bedroom. I jumped up and went into their room to see what was happening. The girls had backed themselves into the corner of their room and they were pointing at the ceiling screaming. When I looked up, I noticed there were these little green geckos hanging from the ceiling. I had forgotten to tell them about those little creatures. They hang out on the ceiling at night and eat the flies. If it were not for those lizards, the flies and mosquitoes would eat us alive. Besides, they would not come close to humans. So I let them move into my room for the night.

The following day, Ronsillaga took us to one of the local villages which had a small church. This was another adjustment for the kids because they had never seen buildings like these.

I was not scheduled to speak that Sunday, but the pastor was not passing up an opportunity to have a guest from the States just sit there. They had three services on Sunday: one in English for the more educated, then another one in Singhalese, and another in Tamil. When I was scheduled to speak in churches, I had to use two different interpreters. That made for a long day. It did not take long for us to realize that Sunday was an all-day event at church.

Ronsillaga and I used the following week traveling so the kids could get aquatinted with the area and the traveling conditions.

It wasn't long before I realized that I needed my own transportation, so I got my driver's license and bought us a van. It only took me a few short weeks to realize that I was not cut out to drive in this environment. There was everything on the road that could move, and there were no rules. When approaching an intersection, you got through the best way you could, *if* there were no traffic police on duty.

The first assignment was an area outreach in Colombo, and that's when the kids did their puppets, which was a big hit! I thought this was a great way to reach the children; however, the grownups loved them even more.

This was a lifetime adventure for the kids. They were experiencing things that their little minds couldn't conceive. They saw kids taking baths in drain ditches and playing in areas that were unsanitary, but through it all, they adjusted. They didn't have any complaints once they moved past living with the geckos hanging around in the house.

Also, all of us had to make some big adjustments in our daily eating habits. We learned to appreciate spicy meals for breakfast, lunch, and dinner. We ate what they cooked when we were in the villages and enjoyed it. We didn't cook and season our own food at home very often because we were on the road so much; therefore, we adjusted to the local villagers' cooking.

We had to make more adjustments in our lifestyle once the school year began. I learned quickly that I could not manage a household in this culture. We had to shop for each meal because there was no frig for storage. We had to cook on a stove that I was not familiar with. There was too much of a change for me to try to deal with the household stuff; so I did what the average working family did: hired myself a housekeeper.

On the mission field, we had to live on a fixed income, so I was concerned about the cost. I shared my needs with my brother in Christ, Ronsillaga, who was quick to respond. He got me a full-time housekeeper and it only cost me 26 rupees a day which was 50 cents a day in American money.

When the kids started school, we encountered another problem: transportation. Again I shared my need with my brother in Christ, and he came through on time. He got me a rickshaw driver to transport the kids to and from school.

Most of the children who attended the international school had private drivers. The little yellow and black rickshaw was another common carrier. It cost me 26 rupees a day (50 cents).

Now I had a full-time housekeeper and a full-time driver, and it only cost me, $1.00 a day for both! Once my house was taken care of, I had peace of mind. Now I could focus on the ministry.

During the day, while the kids were in school, I had visitors coming from all areas of the island. They were pastors, local leaders, and missionaries from the UK, Germany, and the US. When I went on this mission, I didn't realize that the Lord was going to use me as a counselor, a teacher, and a preacher. I committed everything that I did to His authority because I knew that I was functioning in areas in which I had no training. I was just a willing vessel open to whatever the Lord asked me to do.

During the school year, I would follow up with the kids to see how they were progressing in school. They loved it! They said all they had to do was to listen as the teacher talked and wrote things on the board. They didn't use very many books. They compared that style of teaching with the schools back home. They enjoyed going to school, but that was short-lived. It caught up with them when it was time for exams. All of them fell behind because they didn't have any notes to study when the exams came. They fell behind because they didn't pass their quarterly exams, which became a big distraction for me.

My partner came up with a plan: hire a teacher to work with them. He said tutors were common in his country because most kids used them to help during exam time. My next-door neighbor was a teacher, and she was willing to work with them. I offered her 52.00 rupees a day ($1.00). She took leave from the school system and worked for me full time. I noticed a big change in the kids' behavior and attitude toward their school work.

We made it through the first year on the mission field, and I sensed the Lord was preparing us for even greater things during the coming year.

GROWING IN THE LORD

It was New Year's Eve and one local pastor asked if we would participate in their holiday program: An all-night event!

We started about 8 p.m. with songs, praises, and prayer. He had some real prayer warriors among the ladies in his church. The ladies in the Sri Lanka churches were greatly involved in the church service.

This was not the case in India. The regular service started about 11 p.m., and we prayed into the early morning hours. This was the first time that I had ever participated in an all-night service. Most of the children fell asleep on floor mats. I was energized from the music, dance, and prayer.

The ladies of the church served hot tea and light snacks during the breaks. There was a certain lady in the service that night who caught my attention as she prayed and served the people. I couldn't take my eyes off her throughout the night; not in a lustful way. I was intrigued by her prayer life and her attitude of worship. I thought to myself, how blessed is her husband to have a woman with such a strong willingness to serve the Lord. I was taken back to a period when I had a wife, a friend, and a mother for my children.

A few weeks later, I was speaking at another church in that area, and I saw her again. This time I noticed she had two children with her, but I didn't see her husband. After church we enjoyed a time of fellowship, tea and snacks before the afternoon service started. I continued to watch this lady as she interacted with church members, but this wasn't the same church she attended when I first noticed her. She had a very beautiful smile, and she displayed very good social skills, like that of a preacher's wife.

When the afternoon service started, the pastor asked for someone to open in prayer. She stood and started praying, first in English, then in her language Singhalese, then in Tamil. I was touched by her prayers in all three languages. After the service, I asked Sister Mercy, the pastor's wife, who this lady was. She said that she was a local lady from the village.

She went on to explain how much she loved the Lord and was always willing to serve Him. I asked about her husband, to which she replied in a sad tone, "She is a divorcée. Her husband gave her a certificate of divorce a few years ago. He remarried and then moved to the Mideast, leaving her and the kids."

I asked how a woman with her qualities remained single for so long. She replied, "Once a woman becomes a divorcée, no other man will take her for his wife. It would be different if her husband died; then she could remarry, but not a divorcée. She based that on 2nd Corinthians 7 and their culture. However, that was not the teaching in their church.

Weeks passed, and I couldn't get this lady out of my mind. I attended a meeting at one of the mission houses in Colombo. She was there working as a server for the guests. I asked one of the pastors (female) about this lady and her eyes lit up. She smiled and said, "She would make you a great wife. Your children need a mother; her children need a father, and you two would be good in the ministry together!"

Wow, she laid a lot on my heart in a very short time. I asked what about her being a divorcée; isn't that against your teaching? She said that was the teaching and belief of the village churches where she lived. I asked if she would introduce me. She agreed, but we had to stay in public while we talked. She reminded me that we couldn't be alone.

We met and her name was Ranuka. We talked as
we sat in the church court yard during a break in the
meeting. I was surprised. She spoke very good English
along with two other languages. I learned that she had
two kids (girl, boy) the same age as my oldest and
youngest daughters. I learned that she had a brother
who was married, and her mother lived with him.
She went on to tell me they weren't very close. She
was the only Christian in the family, and they blamed

her for the divorce. She went on to explain how her husband was abusive. He beat her, so she took the kids and ran away. That's why she lived with the village people. They didn't bother her as long as she lived as a divorcée. She explained how the Lord had blessed her and her children. She also explained that her children were blessed to attend one of the best government schools on the island. We had a word of prayer and parted.

I learned very quickly: there is no courtship in Sri Lanka as it is in our country. If you wanted to date a lady, first you get her parents' permission. Then you have to explain your intent. If they approve, you still couldn't be alone. You must have a chaperone every place you go.

I got permission from the pastor and his wife to spend time with her after services on Sunday. They agreed and the ladies of the church would gather in small groups, giggling, acting like a bunch of little girls when one of them got a boyfriend.

It didn't take long before I realized in my heart that she would be my wife, but I knew I should talk to my kids and get their input. But first I spoke with the pastor and his wife concerning my intent. His wife sat there with a big grin on her face during our entire conversation. She didn't say a word, but I could tell she agreed with each word, based on the size of her grin. After our conversation, the pastor planned a meal for the following night at their house so I could propose. That was the process if a family were a member of the church, especially a widow or divorcée. The pastor's wife was excited. She committed our plans to the Lord and ended in prayer.

I went home that evening and told the kids about this lady. They knew right away whom I was speaking of. They knew her kids, and they were about to ask me if they could come over and spend the day when I went out of town the next week. I agreed to their request and I told them about my plans for our future. They hit the ceiling with shouts of joy!! They had already talked among themselves about my getting them a mother from Sri Lanka. They were so excited after I explained the details of my plans!!

I went to bed that night thinking: "This has to be from God; the joy from the pastor's wife and now with my four children." This was the confirmation I needed to help me sleep that night.

The following day I met with my missionary partners. After all, a few of them had proposed one of their family members as a wife and mother for the children. I met the ladies at their family homes, but I didn't feel the leading from the Lord. I was not going to venture out and marry a woman, especially from another country on my own. I wanted the Lord to open the door. Now I felt that He had done that with Ranuka.

The kids and I arrived at the pastor's house a bit early because I wanted to get the kids settled with the other kids for their time of fellowship.

I learned very quickly that the pastor's wife didn't understand the meaning of confidentiality.

When we arrived, I could tell most of the ladies in the church already knew why I was there and that included Ranuka. They were walking the courtyard whispering, looking at me grinning like a bunch of grade-school girls.

When we sat for dinner that evening, the pastor got right to the point. "Sister Ranuka, Brother Lee wants to propose marriage. Will you accept?"

Everyone could tell that she was happy with that proposal based on her smile. She said, "Yes!

She asked, "Pastor, is he aware that I am a divorcée, and I have two children?" The Pastor acknowledged and he explained that it wouldn't be an issue in his church. She turned and asked me, "Do you think that I will make you a good wife?" I could tell by her questions that her confidence level was at an all-time low.

Then she asked in a very soft tone, "Will you beat me if I do something wrong?"

At that point, the pastor's wife spoke up on my behalf and assured her that I would be good to her and her children.

Ranuka wanted to know where we would live. I told her that I had a house in Colombo that was large enough for the two families. We would live there, and I would provide a driver to transport the kids to school.

She asked to be excused. She and the pastor's wife went out into the courtyard, and they talked for a while. The Pastor explained that I was a foreigner, and she did not know very much about the lifestyle of outsiders.

We prayed to seek the guidance from the Lord. Pastor explained, "If God is in this, all will go well."

When we came back together, we were engaged. All six kids were so excited.

We planned to start the paperwork process the following day and get married the following Saturday. She had never been involved in this process before because the man's family took care of these details.

But I told her I wanted to start our relationship by doing things together. She was a bit apprehensive but agreed after the pastor's wife gave her nod and a smile.

It took us only a few hours to get our marriage license. (That's because I paid the clerk a bribe on the spot.) Sri Lanka is a very corrupt country. I learned that back in the day when I got my driver's license.

The next step: I told her I wanted to meet her family. She was not sold on that idea because they weren't very close since her divorce. They blamed her for the break up. We stopped at a roadside tea shop where we had some tea. I convinced her it was the right thing to do even if they disapproved. She agreed, reluctantly.

When we arrived at her brother's house, he wasn't home from work, but her mother was there. She welcomed us with open arms. They started talking about a mile a minute in their language. I couldn't understand a word they were saying, but I could tell they were talking about me. Then the conversation came to a point where Mom stood up and gave me a big hug. She started talking to me in broken English, but I managed to understand every word she said. I was sure she was happy with the marriage. I was hoping we would get the same reception from her brother and sister-in-law.

When her brother arrived home, he made me feel welcome with a warm smile and a firm hand shake. The same welcome came from the sister-in-law. I felt right at home, and Ranuka had reunited with her family.

Brother and sister-in-law spoke very good English. He owned a tourist business, and she was a bank auditor. We spent hours talking about how we met and our plans for the future and the work going on in the ministry in the outlying areas of the Island.

My brother-in-law cautioned me about working in the outlying areas because he had first-hand knowledge of the fighting that was going on in the hill country and villages.

Ranuka and her family's relationships were growing closer every day. After a few months, her mother moved in with us, and she became the cook. All of us loved her cooking.

All the kids were getting along and learning about each others' likes and dislikes. Her kids were experiencing a freedom of speech like never before. They loved the way my kids were able to talk openly and debate about job duties that I asked them to do. It was like being in a meeting room at dinner. All of them were talking about their day and the events that took place in school.

The work that I was doing with the villagers was getting a lot of attention from the local government. Some of the officials visited the work sites and tried to encourage me to give them a cut of the money that we were spending on labor and supplies. I refused.

One day when I came home, there were some State Officials along with a group of Military Police. The police were staged on the roof and in the front yard. They had Ranaka and the kids held in the room in the corners with machine guns pointing at them.

When I walked into the house, the State Official was sitting at the table, and my mother-in-law was serving him and his men lunch. I got very upset when I saw them.

My first response was; "What are you doing in my house? You don't have any right to be in my home!"

The State Official jumped up from the table. With a mouth filled with food, he responded, "THIS IS MY COUNTRY! *YOU* DON'T HAVE ANY RIGHTS!"

After he said that, he smiled as he continued to chew with a month full of food. He invited me to sit down at the table and have something to eat. He continued to talk and eat using only his hand as a utensil.

He made a proposal: "I will permit you to continue working in the villages without any problems from the local government official, but it will cost you 12000 rupees ($200.00) a month."

When he made that statement, I responded, "ARE-YOU OUT OF YOUR MIND?!"

I learned very quickly that was not the right thing to say. He spoke to his men in their native language. The police grabbed my wife and her mother and pushed them into the corner and to their knees. They had their guns pointed in their faces. My wife and mother-in-law began to cry and beg for mercy in their own language.

He said that he would expect his full payment at the first of each month.

My wife and her mother were very upset even after they left and into the evening. Her mother caught a cab and went to her son's house.

Ranuka and I talked about the possibility of leaving the country, but she wasn't sure because she and her children had never been off the island. She cried most of the night. The kids were quiet and fearful. We had a family prayer time that evening.

THE WORK CONTINUES

The following day when I got to the village, I shared what had happened concerning the visit from the government office with Ronsillaga.

It didn't shock him any because he knew how his government worked. He suggested we continue to work. I was frustrated concerning his request. After all, we could build a new home with what this state official was asking me to pay him.

The first of the month deadline the government official had given me to pay had passed.

The villagers were very happy to see that outsiders cared more about their needs than their own government did.

The other missionaries were having great success in the areas they were working. They had constructed several feeding centers and a medical center all centrally located with easy access for the villages and the receiving of supplies.

The Lord was blessing everything we put our hands on. Numbers were added to the local churches, and people were being baptized daily.

The leaders in the village where I was working wanted to show their appreaciation for the work we were doing by having a festival. They were so excited about the progress.

They even invited the Buddhist Priest. Some things that I learned about the Buddhist Priest were that they loved the attention of outsiders, and they loved to eat.

All the villages and the missionaries came together for this fun-time event. The ladies cooked a bunch of food, mostly vegetables, meat, and fish. Most of the villagers were not accustomed to eating this type of meal with all the meat and fish because of the cost factor. The festival lasted into the late afternoon. I thought it was best to start home before dark, because traveling after dark was not advised because of the wild animals.

That's when it happened. About 5 jeeps filled with police officers and one with two government officials drove up. They surrounded the area where we were and pulled their machine guns.

The Government Official who visited my house a few weeks back motioned for all the missionaries to come over to his jeep. We complied.

He told us that the government was revoking our visas. We had to leave the country immediately. He motioned for us to get into his jeep, and they drove us away. We thought that we were being escorted home to pack and get our family. Instead, they took us straight to the airport.

We protested about leaving our family behind, but he didn't hear a word we were saying. They escorted us into the airport and put us out of the country. We had learned early that we should always carry our passports and other documents with us at all times. Therefore, we had everything we needed to return home, but we were more concerned about our families.

We caught the first flight leaving the country going to Saudi Arabia where we got connecting flights to

England and on to the US. We were so caught up in this situation, we didn't even pray. All of us were lost for words.

I cannot begin to put into words my feelings and the loneliness that I was going through during those 39 hours coming back to the States without my family.

We didn't have the phone system as we have it today. There was no way that any of us could contact our family and let them know what had happened.

When I landed in LAX, I felt like a wrestler who had just finished a 10-round fight. My body was hot, sweaty, and my clothes were dirty from the work in the village. I'm sure I had a body odor based on the expression of everyone around me. If they only knew: body odor was the least of my concerns.

When I boarded the flight from LAX to St. Louis, I was sandwiched between two women. One of the ladies worked for a St. Louis newspaper.

Based on my appearance and body odor, I felt that I owed them an explanation. When I started talking, I had the attention of everyone seated around us.

When I arrived in St. Louis, the newspaper lady made an appointment to meet me the following day at the apartment in the rear of the church in Glenn Carbon, IL, where I was staying. She came over that morning with her film crew to interview me.

The following Sunday, this article appeared in the *St. Louis Post Dispatch*. She even gave me the title: Rev. Leroy Cannady.

A family portrait taken before their journey to Sri Lanka showing the Rev. Leroy Kennedy and his four American-born children. From left: Bobby, Amber, Christina and Michael.

Visa Problems Splinter Family

I was lost for words because I didn't know how I was going to get my family home from Sri Lanka.

One night during my time of prayer and devotion, (12/10/91) I opened my Bible at random and read the following Scripture:

"Do not be afraid, for I am with you, I will bring your children from the east and gather you from the west. I will say to the north, 'Give them up!' And to the south, 'Do not hold them back.' Bring my sons from afar and my daughters from the ends of the earth--- Everyone who is called by my name whom I created for my glory, whom I formed and made." (Isaiah. 43:5-7 NIV)

After reading that scripture, the peace of God came all over me. I realized there wasn't anything that I could do to get my family home. It was in the hands of the Lord.

It took the American Embassy six months to negotiate a deal so I could return to Sri Lanka and get my children. I was told that I had 48 hours to get in and get out. We didn't have any complication with our departure. It took another three months to get my new wife and her children.

After we returned to the States, we settled in the children's hometown of Edwardsville, IL, which was close to where their mother and twin sisters were laid to rest.

Conclusion:

Sometime later, I visited Battle Creek, Michigan, much like that park where I had my powerful encounter with the Lord Jesus Christ years ago. It took me hours driving through the streets of Battle Creek, trying to locate that park and that park bench.

Finally, I located the park, and the activities were still the same as years earlier.

I parked and walked slowly toward the pond where they feed the ducks. Then I saw it! The bench was still there. Some repairs had been made, but the foundation had not moved.

I stared at the bench for a moment, and then the peace of God came over me. That was my confirmation that I was in the right place. I walked around the bench several times and looked at the surrounding area. There was no doubt that I had made it back where it had all begun.

I sat down on that bench, and my tears began to fall. My tears were flowing heavily. My sight was blurry. My life at that moment began to replay.

I thought about my state of mind during those days and the thoughts about taking my life. I remember how my thoughts of suicide, my attitude of bitterness, greed, emptiness, and my dependence on drugs changed in an instant when I prayed and asked Jesus Christ to come into my heart and be my Lord and Savior.

I began to praise Him! "Lord, you repaired my marriage; you blessed us with four children after doctors said it was impossible. You delivered me from the drugs, the alcohol, and cigarettes. You repaired my career and blessed us financially. You called us to serve as a team in The Gideons International.

The enemy got control of my thoughts for a moment, and I shifted quickly, and started focusing on the negatives of my past: The stabbing death of my father; the death of my mother at the age of forty-eight from alcohol; my drug addiction; husband of three wives at age of thirty; the death of my wife from cancer, leaving me with four young children! My blessing from our sub-division turned into a curse! My time on the mission field resulted in my being separated from my children for six months, and I had to leave my new wife and her two children behind for nine months.

The negative thoughts were getting the best of me. I stood up and walked around that bench holding my head. I tried to get those thoughts out of my head, but the negativity of my past was still getting the best of me.

I looked up and called upon the Name of the Lord, and then He spoke to my heart with scripture references:

"I GAVE YOU MY WORD YEARS AGO THE LAST TIME YOU SAT ON THIS BENCH." Isaiah 1:19

"I GAVE YOU MY WORD WHEN I BROUGHT CHARLOTTE (your wife) HOME FOR MY GLORY," Romans 8:28

"I GAVE YOU MY WORD WHEN YOU WERE SEPARATED FROM YOUR CHILDREN IN SRI LANKA," Isaiah 43:5-7

"NOW, I AM GIVING YOU MY WORD TO CLOSE THIS MATTER OF DOUBT!"

"BEFORE THE FOUNDATION OF THE WORLD, I KNEW YOU AND CALLED YOU BY NAME FOR MY PURPOSE."

"IF YOU DO NOT STAND FIRM IN YOUR FAITH, YOU WILL NOT STAND AT ALL!" Isaiah 7:9b

"REMEMBER YE NOT THE FORMER THINGS, NEITHER CONSIDER THE THINGS OF OLD. BEHOLD, I WILL DO A NEW THING; NOW IT SHALL SPRING FORTH; SHALL YE NOT KNOW IT? I WILL EVEN MAKE A WAY IN THE WILDERNESS, AND RIVERS IN THE DESERT." Isaiah 43:18-20

LORD, FORGIVE ME FOR MY WEAKNESS AND DOUBT DURING TRYING TIMES!

My closing prayer: Lord, I WILL GO WHERE YOU WANT ME TO GO; I WILL DO WHAT YOU ASK ME TO DO; AND I WILL BE WHAT YOU REQUIRE ME TO BE!!! I AM YOURS!